"*Finally, a book on asset protection that is easy and interesting to read. Mr. Reed's personal story leading him to the asset protection business is delightful. He describes in simple terms how anyone can afford to protect their assets from the litigation juggernaut. This book makes it abundantly clear that asset protection is no longer reserved only for the rich and famous. It is and should be available to anyone.*"

David R. Fletcher, LL.B. (Hons)
Nassau, Bahamas

"*Corporations are well-known to those of us in the private banking business. Banking secrecy is a well-established precept of our financial system. **Bulletproof Asset Protection** is a very good book for anyone wanting to know how to protect their assets from lawyers and unwelcome government agencies.*"

Jean-Philippe Bodevin
Private Banking
Liechtenstein

"*As a corporate lawyer, I deal with the many benefits a corporation can provide for my clients. The shield from personal liability and the tax advantages alone make incorporation viable in most cases. But **Bulletproof Asset Protection** will teach you wealth management and preservation that is light years beyond just simple incorporation. This book is a must read for anyone wishing to peer into twenty-first century money management.*"

Dirk A. Ravenholt, Esq.

"*I have known and worked with Mr. Reed for almost ten years. No one knows more about Nevada and offshore corporations. His asset protection strategies are simple and direct. This book should be of interest to anyone interested in assembling an asset protection plan, especially U.S. citizens.*"

MaLou Wittman
Account Manager
Brussels, Belgium

BULLETPROOF
ASSET
PROTECTION

BULLETPROOF
A$$ET
PROTECTION

WILLIAM S. REED, J.D.

INTERNATIONAL FREE PRESS

AUTHOR:	William S. Reed, J.D.
FRONT COVER DESIGN:	Steven Coxson
	William S. Reed
LAYOUT & DESIGN:	H. Donald Kroitzsh

Printed in the United States of America

Published by:
International Free Press
4601 W. Sahara Ave., Suite I
Las Vegas, NV 89102   USA

Prepared by:
Five Corners Press
Plymouth, Vermont 05056   USA

Bulletproof Asset Protection
ISBN: 0-9718734-0-2 (Previously ISBN 1-886699-24-0)
2nd Edition, 1st Printing
Business/Personal Finance

For Jack and Kirk

CONTENTS

INTRODUCTION

"If you love wealth better than liberty, the tranquility of servitude better than the animating contest of freedom, go home from us in peace. We ask not your counsels or arms. Crouch down and lick the hands which feed you. May your chains set lightly upon you, and may posterity forget that you were our countrymen."

– Samuel Adams
Philadelphia State House
August, 1, 1776

"Guard with jealous attention the public liberty. Suspect everyone who approaches that jewel. Unfortunately, nothing will preserve it but downright force. Whenever you give up that force, you are ruined. The great object is, that every man be armed. . . that everyone who is able may have a gun."

– Patrick Henry
Virginia ratification convention
1787

"The condition upon which God hath given liberty to man is eternal vigilance."

– Irish statesman John Philpot Curran

"Grave threats to liberty often come in times of urgency, when constitutional rights seem too extravagant to endure."

– Justice Thurgood Marshall

"Good intentions will always be pleaded for any assumption of power. The constitution was made to guard the people against the dangers of good intentions. There are men in all ages who mean to govern well, but they mean to govern. They promise to be good masters, but they mean to be masters."

– Daniel Webster

Our constitutionally guaranteed rights are under attack, not from some threatening outside force, but from our own government – and our own people. For instance, the First Amendment Center at Vanderbilt University conducted a survey during February and March of 1999 and found that 53 percent of those questioned believe that the press has too much freedom. That's an increase of 15 percentage points from 1997.

"It's a humbling reminder that fundamental rights of expression can disappear if the press and public are not vigilant," said Ken Paulson, the center's executive director.

The survey was conducted to explore Americans' commitment to the forty-five word First Amendment that guarantees freedoms of religion, speech, the press, petition, and assembly. The poll identified freedom of speech as one of the most cherished of constitutional rights, followed by freedom of religion and the Second Amendment's right to bear arms. Nevertheless, when asked to name any of the specific rights guaranteed by the First Amendment, 49 percent of those questioned could not.

On October 26, 2001, President Bush signed the "Uniting and Strengthening America by Providing Appropriate Tools Required to Intercept and Obstruct Terrorism Act" commonly called the USA Patriot Act into law. This federal law gives all domestic federal law enforcement agencies and international intelligence agencies sweeping new powers. It sweeps away all checks and balances applicable to federal courts going back to the revelations in 1974 that the FBI and foreign agencies had spied on over 10,000 citizens, including John F. Kennedy and Martin Luther King.

The law is over 342 pages long and makes changes to over fifteen different statutes. As Laura W. Murphy, Director of the ACLU's Washington National Office stated: "This law is based on the faulty assumption that safety must come at the expense of civil liberties. The USA Patriot Act gives law enforcement agencies nationwide extraordinary new powers unchecked by meaningful judicial review."

Many provisions of the Bill of Rights have been dismantled by this Act. The Act is a direct threat to our civil liberties and what remains of our right to privacy. It continues the relentless trend of granting federal courts and government agencies increased access to personal financial information rather than attempting to prevent further intrusions. The law requires financial institutions to monitor daily transactions more closely and share information with any federal agency such as the IRS, including foreign intelligence services such as the CIA and the U.S. Customs Service. It effectively puts the CIA back in the business of spying on Americans. Unknown to most citizens, the law allows law enforcement agencies to secretly acquire individual credit reports. The law does not require or provide for judicial review and does not mandate that the person whose records are being reviewed be given any notice.

Just a few of the USA Patriot Act's most troubling provisions that threaten our personal liberties and invade our privacy are listed below:

1. It grants the FBI broad access to sensitive business records about individuals without having to show evidence of a crime.

2. The law expands all four traditional tools of surveillance including wiretaps, search warrants, pen/trap orders and subpoenas. A pen/trap order requires the telephone company to reveal the numbers dialed to and from a particular phone. Their counterparts under the Foreign Intelligence Surveillance Act (FISA) that allow spying *in the U.S.* by foreign intelligence agencies have similarly been expanded.

3. The Act extends the authority of the government to mandate "secret searches" far beyond anything necessary to conduct terrorism investigations.

4. The Act allows law enforcement agencies to conduct "roving" wiretaps. This form of wiretap allows electronic surveillance of an individual

rather than a specific telephone, cell phone or computer terminal. Congress and the President have effectively amended or eliminated some of the personal freedoms enunciated in the Fourth Amendment pertaining to limiting government search and seizure warrants. They did this without the consent of the people, as required by the Constitution.

5. It allows law enforcement agencies increased surveillance powers over telephone conversations and Internet communications.

6. The government has the power to secretly investigate any citizen for "intelligence" purposes.

7. The Act takes a bite out of the traditional attorney-client privilege rules. It allows government agents to monitor conversations between people in federal custody and their lawyers if the attorney general, at his sole discretion, deems it "reasonably necessary in order to deter future acts of violence or terrorism."

8. In a direct threat to the free speech provision of the First Amendment, the Act provides that a lawful permanent U.S. resident who makes a controversial speech that the *government deems* to be supportive of terrorism can be barred from returning to his or her family after taking a trip abroad.

As frightening as the Act is itself, what's more ominous is the willingness of most Americans to go along with this abridgement of their freedoms. A Harris

Interactive poll taken in late September, 2001, showed 81% favor closer monitoring of banking and credit card transactions; 68% favor implementation of a national ID card; and 63% favor expanded government monitoring of all Internet communications and cell phone conversations. "People are concerned about safety now and will put up with more invasions of privacy," concedes Richard Smith, former CTO of the Privacy Foundation.

Senator Russell Feingold of Wisconsin offered the only criticism of the Act in his thoughtful presentation to Congress. Under withering criticism including people questioning his patriotism, he bravely stated that, "The new law goes into a lot of areas that have nothing to do with terrorism and have a lot go do with the government and the FBI having a wish list of things they want to do, whether it be getting into people's computer use, financial records, or other areas not related to terrorism."

The Senator concluded by pointing out that the Patriot Act highlights the march of technology and its ability to cut both for and against personal liberty. He left Congress with the prophetic statement by Justice Brandeis in a dissenting opinion issued in 1928:

"The progress of science in furnishing the Government with means of espionage is not likely to stop with wire-tapping. Ways may some day be developed by which the Government, without removing papers from secret drawers, can reproduce them in Court, and by which it will be enabled to expose to a jury the most intimate occurrences of the home. Can it be that the Constitution affords no protection against such invasions of individual security?"

The Litigation Explosion

Another method of redistributing the wealth is to file a lawsuit and ask the court system to assist you. The rising tide of frivolous litigation filed by plaintiffs and their lawyers has created an omnipresent threat to anyone with a positive net worth.

One in three Americans will be involved in a lawsuit sometime in their life. The staggering cost in attorneys' fees to defend a lawsuit is many times more onerous than the potential outcome of the lawsuit itself. In the past, lawsuits were filed when a point of law needed to be clarified or the amount of a damage claim needed to be decided by a jury, but that's changed. Because judges lack the backbone to assess plaintiffs and their lawyers for attorneys' fees sustained by the defendants in frivolous or groundless lawsuits, there are legions of underemployed lawyers who have turned a lawsuit into a live hand grenade. They roll it into a room full of defendants and see who will pay.

There is no purer form of extortion than a lawsuit; the defendant has to decide whether to pay the plaintiff or pay his attorney to defend the case. Oh, sure, every state bar association pays lip service to enforcing a code of professional responsibility allegedly designed to restrain its members from filing unfounded lawsuits, but the real story lies in the chilling statistics showing the alarming increase in the number of lawsuits filed each year.

When I started in this business more than twelve years ago, I had never heard the words asset protection to describe a specific field of business. It isn't that people were poorer back then or that wealthy people didn't want to protect their wealth, but with the explosion in litigation, the increasing number of new lawyers, and the construction of new law schools, litigation has become a blood sport used to employ the overpopulation of lawyers.

Nowadays, there is absolutely no moral compass involved with a lawyer's decision to file a lawsuit. Judges have the power to check this trend, but they are all lawyers themselves with a self-interest in perpetuating the system. Congress has the power to limit lawsuits, but most members of Congress are lawyers as well. And if they're not, they feast on the campaign contributions of lawyers and their special interest groups.

Ironically, collection lawyers, government agencies such as the IRS, and everyone outside the asset protection business, make every effort to characterize asset protection as dishonest, fraudulent, or worse. Of course, their motives are transparent. They denounce anyone who successfully thwarts their efforts to collect or seize assets, disrupting the stream of income flowing in their direction. And they do more than talk.

The American Trial Lawyers Association is a brutally powerful and influential private interest group that generously supports any candidate, usually a Democrat, who helps them keep the ground rules of litigation tilted in their favor. They will fight for their right to litigate at all costs. Litigation is their life blood. Be damned the innocent parties who stand in their way.

The Wealth Factor

Up until the 1980s, you had to be a Rockefeller, Ford, or Kennedy to be considered a wealthy person. With the advent of the personal computer industry in the 1980s, the tripling of the value of the stock market in the 1990s, and the never-ending expansion of the federal government's seizure powers, the number of people needing and wanting asset protection has grown exponentially.

As a result, asset protection has become a growth industry. Increasingly, people with wealth or even a modest nest egg must come to terms with the fact that the threat from the federal government or a frivolous lawsuit is real.

I don't pretend to know what the current definition of a wealthy person might be, but I know for certain, as a former collection lawyer, that there have never been so many collectible defendants.

The Peace of Mind Factor

There are also people who will never be sued or be the subject of any investigation. They may have quietly inherited their money or passively invested their assets wisely. They live modestly and spend prudently. No doubt, some people would argue the members of this group needn't worry about or invest in asset protection.

Nevertheless, at least one-third of my clients fall into this category. They're not concerned about divorce or the IRS; they just like to know at least some of their assets are out of sight. They're not doomsday prophets hoarding briefcases full of gold coins; they just derive some comfort in the knowledge that part of their net worth is outside the grasp of the U.S. court system.

I call it bulletproof asset protection. They call it peace of mind.

W. S. R.

CHAPTER 1
IS ASSET PROTECTION AVAILABLE TO EVERYONE

I grew up in a rural setting in the state of North Dakota. It shares its northern border with Canada, so it gets cold there. With long, windchill winters, a sparse population, and no sizable cities, people tend to be self-sufficient. I was always taught that each person had a duty to take care of himself and protect his family. Farmers and ranchers grind out a living working the land or raising livestock. They view lawyers and governments as Thomas Jefferson did, as "necessary evils." They're law abiding citizens (Republican, mostly), but they resent government intrusion with a fervor. The welfare rolls are short, and the unemployment rates are low. The farmers live with the uncertainty of bad weather that can ruin a year's work. There are no ocean views, balmy beaches, or picturesque mountains. As Mark Twain used to say, they're the kind of people that "make do." In other words, they not only believe in the Bill of Rights, they also live the Bill of Rights. Free speech, the right to assemble, and the right to bear arms are all part of their lifestyle.

> THE FEDERAL GOVERNMENT IS SOMETHING TO BE TOLERATED, NOT REVERED.

Individual freedom is not only paramount, it's one of their few luxuries. The federal government is something to be tolerated, not revered.

In the 1960s, I left North Dakota to attend college and law school. The Vietnam war was raging and my fundamental distrust of the government made me a natural leader to protest our involvement. As much as the war, we distrusted the government's leader, Richard Nixon. In 1968, he ran for President on the platform that he would withdraw our troops and end the war. He lied. After getting elected, he announced we could not have peace "without honor." So, he escalated the war (remember his "incursion" into Cambodia in 1970 causing the Kent State imbroglio) causing tens of thousands of additional casualties. In the fall of 1970, he substituted a lottery system for the military draft in hopes of deflating the anti-war movement. To some extent the ploy worked. People like myself who drew high lottery numbers were allowed to walk away from the fighting and the possibility of having to move to Canada. Of course, we eventually lost the war entirely in humiliating fashion. Everyone remembers the grainy footage of desperate Americans scrambling to the roof of the U.S. Embassy to hastily board helicopters as the Viet Cong rode into the city on their tanks rejoicing in victory.

Eventually, everyone's suspicions about Nixon's integrity were proven true. After his impending impeachment and resignation, only a career ending pardon from his successor, Gerald Ford, prevented him from going to prison. Moreover, when the infamous White House tapes were ultimately released, Nixon's paranoid tirades were revealed in their unvarnished state.

With this as a backdrop, I graduated from law school in 1975 and opened my law practice as a sole practitioner. Business was slow, so I tended bar five nights a week to make ends meet. As you might imagine, I defended drunk drivers and got a lot of divorce work. One of my customers owned a large company that managed apartment buildings and other rental properties. He figured I'd work cheap and appreciate having any work at all. He was right. I was introduced to the world of evictions and collections. Over the next fifteen years I developed a legal machine that specialized in processing county court eviction and collection cases.

> I LEARNED FIRSTHAND FROM THE DEFENDANT-DEBTORS HOW TO PROTECT ASSETS FROM A COURT JUDGMENT.

We garnished paychecks, seized bank accounts, liened houses, and snatched automobiles. As the years marched by, I learned firsthand from the defendant-debtors how to protect assets from a court judgment. I had never heard the words "asset protection," I just knew some debtors were careful not to have anything in their own name, to make sure their wife owned the house and that their other assets were held by a corporation. We were handling over 1,000 cases a month, so when we got a judgment and couldn't garnish a paycheck, seize a bank account, or lien a house, we dropped it and moved on to more collectible cases. Most collectors recover between ten and thirty cents on every dollar owed and we were no different. Volume was the key. Lots of cases, dump the difficult ones, press hard where there were assets. Business was good, the karma was bad.

With the passage of the 1986 Tax Reform Act and the subsequent collapse of the banking industry, many of my wealthy real estate clients lost their apartment buildings to foreclosure and were sued when the buildings sold for less than the mortgage amount. That was 1988. They came and implored me, "Bill, where can we put our money where it's safe?" So I went to the library (that's the building we used to go to before the Internet) and discovered the fledgling world of asset protection. In 1990, I appeared in court for the last time. I traveled to dozens of countries to learn first hand the mechanics of asset protection and which jurisdictions specialized in helping Americans protect their assets from lawsuits and governmental agencies. It was the best decision I ever made.

> "BILL, WHERE CAN WE PUT OUR MONEY WHERE IT'S SAFE?"

For over twelve years I've been helping people protect their assets from lawsuits, lawyers, or worse. And although it generally goes unspoken, most people wonder if protecting their assets from private lawyers and the government is legal and (dare I say) moral. With regard to the legal question, the short answer is, "Yes, it's legal."

It's interesting to note that most people understand why wealthy, English rock stars renounce their homeland to protect their assets. No one was shocked when the grandsons of eccentric billionaire oil tycoon John Paul Getty renounced their U.S. citizenship and became tax refugees by becoming Irish citizens. Or that Madonna, Michael Jackson, or O.J. Simpson have used corporations to shield their wealth from creditors. In the United States, we have a double standard when it comes to asset protection. When wealthy, famous, or powerful people protect their assets it's called "financial planning," but when everyday people like the rest of us move our assets out of the reach of lawyers, it's called "defrauding our creditors." And, if an arm of the federal government is involved, such as the IRS or the U.S. Customs Service, they'll describe your activities as a form of

> **Asset protection is not a privilege, it is a freedom protected by the Constitution.**

"money laundering." Asset protection is not a privilege, it is a freedom protected by the Constitution. However, as the late film maker Samuel Goldwyn once said, "Timing is everything."

Don't wait until you're a defendant in a lawsuit or the target of an IRS investigation to consider protecting your assets. If a creditor has a legitimate claim against an identifiable asset, it may be against the law to transfer or sell that asset. Most states endorse the Uniform

> **Timing is everything.**

Fraudulent Conveyance Act that prohibits a debtor from transferring his assets with the intent to hinder, delay, or defraud a known creditor. You've got to protect yourself before the storm approaches, not in the middle of it.

A few years ago, a young, smart plastic surgeon came to my office to ask about asset protection. At the time, he didn't have any assets. In fact, he was in debt for his student loans and other expenses incurred while he learned to be a doctor. But he had recently joined a medical group of other plastic surgeons and was confident about his financial future.

We formed two Nevada corporations and one offshore corporation to own or mortgage any real estate he had and to hold any other liquid assets he intended to acquire. As the years ticked by, my client bought a house, leased a new Mercedes, and set up an offshore stock brokerage account. He maintained each of his corporations, keeping them in good standing, and always used me as his nominee officer and director.

A few months ago we had lunch and he showed me a thick stack of legal pleadings naming him as one of the defendants. The plaintiff was a disgruntled patient of one of the other surgeons in the medical group. Her breast enlargement wasn't big enough, allegedly causing her pain and suffering, emotional distress, and a dysfunctional sex life. Although my client had never even seen this patient, her lawyers were careful to name all the doctors in the group, hoping for a larger settlement.

Although the medical group carried liability insurance, each of the doctors still had some potential personal liability. Further, the more the insurance company was required to pay, the more their premiums would go up. My friend went on to explain that before any answer or responsive pleading was filed, his attorney explained to plaintiff's counsel that he had no assets. Counsel for the plaintiff laughed and turned the matter over to a private investigator. After searching the Internet, real estate and banking records, and obtaining a complete credit report, counsel for the plaintiff grudgingly was forced to admit that my client owned nothing. The case against my client was quietly dropped.

His timing and foresight were impeccable. To this day he carries on as a plastic surgeon with a minimum of malpractice insurance, doing the work he genuinely loves.

The other unspoken question surrounding asset protection goes something like this, "All right, it's legal, but if I do this am I some kind of cheater or shyster?" In other words, people are concerned that they will be accused of abiding by the same moral code practiced by most members of the legal profession if they shield their assets from the courts. Without delving into any kind of philosophical or religious discussion of morals, I can only say that once you have accumulated assets, you can be sure any money-hungry lawyer or federal government agency will not allow any moral code to dampen their enthusiasm for seizing your cash.

Here are just a few of the areas where your wealth may be threatened:

1. Divorce. Marriage is a beautiful thing, but it works only about half the time. A prenuptial agreement is a good idea, but the courts routinely fail to uphold them. Recently, the California Supreme Court set aside the prenuptial agreement signed by a wealthy baseball player and his wife on the grounds that "she wasn't sure she knew what she was doing," even though she was represented by counsel at all times. Your best protection is to establish a separate, private financial life that is known only to you. The price of falling in love shouldn't include the loss of all your assets when the flame dies.

> MARRIAGE IS A BEAUTIFUL THING, BUT IT WORKS ONLY ABOUT HALF THE TIME.

2. Taxes. An IRS tax audit may leave you with a large assessment for taxes, penalties, and interest that you are unable to pay and that are not dischargeable in bankruptcy. The cost of challenging the IRS in court is prohibitively expensive for most people, and your assets are frozen if you choose to grind your case through the court system. Better to have your assets where the IRS can never seize them or know about them.

> YOUR BEST PROTECTION IS TO ESTABLISH A SEPARATE, PRIVATE FINANCIAL LIFE THAT IS KNOWN ONLY TO YOU.

3. Medical expenses. Unanticipated medical bills for you or a family member that are not covered by your health insurance policy or HMO can become staggering. As a collection attorney, I knew the best debts to take to court involved unpaid medical bills. The debtor, or a member of his family, could rarely argue they never contracted for or received the services. If the debtor didn't go bankrupt, we'd get 25 percent of his paycheck until we were paid.

4. Negligence lawsuits. These can be filed by the customers of your business as the result of the activities of your employees. Your delivery driver that gets drunk and slams into a school bus is your responsibility. Oh, I know, we all carry insurance, but what if your limits aren't high enough or the insurance company refuses to pay?

5. Uninsured motorists. In an automobile accident with an uninsured motorist when the damages exceed your insurance policy limits, you may have to pay the difference.

6. Sexual harassment suits or other claims filed against you as an employer. This is a growing area of litigation, which favors the plaintiffs.

7. A failed business venture. Your former best friend, business partner, and confidante becomes your newest worst enemy. IRS agents have stated on numerous occasions that the primary source of independent informers on tax cheats are ex-wives or girlfriends and ex-business partners. And as anyone with a family business knows, blood is not always thicker than water.

> As anyone with a family business knows, blood is not always thicker than water.

8. Loan guarantees. You sign as a personal guarantor for a loan to a family member or friend. The loan goes into default and the lender sues you.

9. Currently, the fastest growing threat to your wealth is the federal government. Between the years of 1985 and 1995, government seizures increased by 2,000 percent according to a congressional report. Yet, according to government watchdog groups, 80 percent of those who have had their property seized were never charged with any crime. The government knows most people can't afford to challenge the onerous legal machinations of a federal agency. The notion of innocent until proven guilty has been turned upside down.

Any U.S. citizen with property or financial assets located in the United States should be aware of the threat of civil asset forfeiture, especially in light of the Patriot Act discussed earlier. Over the past twenty years, the federal government has quietly increased its police power to confiscate your real and personal property. All they have to do is allege that the target asset was somehow used or involved in some ambiguous criminal activity and the asset can be seized without notice. You may be tempted to dismiss this threat as something reserved only for drug dealers, money-laundering criminals, and terrorists, but I urge you to beware.

There are currently over a hundred different federal forfeiture statutes designed to cover any kind of misconduct, whether it be criminal or civil. For instance, a woman in Los Angeles had her car confiscated after the police arrested her husband in the car with a prostitute. (As if she hadn't suffered enough.)

In Las Vegas in the summer of 1998, the U.S. Customs Service seized twenty-four checking accounts from a local bank without any notice or due process of law. Eighteen of the accounts belonged to innocent victims who had nothing to do with the U.S. Customs investigation. Nevertheless, they were forced to spend tens of thousands of dollars on attorney's fees in an attempt to recover their money. In this case, with one affidavit from one customs agent, the customs service was able to obtain a seizure warrant signed by a federal judge in the Southern District of New York, allowing them to seize the accounts without any notice or hearing of any kind. An isolated case? Maybe.

> THE U.S. CUSTOMS SERVICE SEIZED TWENTY-FOUR CHECKING ACCOUNTS FROM A LOCAL BANK WITHOUT ANY NOTICE OR DUE PROCESS OF LAW.

In 1988, when I was still a practicing collection attorney, I had lunch with a grizzled old federal judge. With wiry grey hair and the build of an NFL linebacker, he was an ominous figure even without the imposing title of federal judge. We were trading war stories about the collection business and ruminating over the fact that the people with the most money were the hardest from which to collect. I explained that sometimes a crafty debtor could transfer his assets out of his name, making them hard to attach. At that time, Family Limited Partnerships and Trusts were being touted as ironclad asset protection devices, even though we routinely convinced judges to pierce them, allowing my clients to seize the assets.

As we cut into our charred, medium-rare filet mignon, the judge let out sort of a grunt. Not a laugh. Just one of those grunts that warns a trial lawyer that his legs are about to be cut off at the knees. Federal judges don't make big money, but they make up for it in power, prestige, and their ability to deliver pain. And every one of their orders is backed up and enforced by the full weight of the federal law enforcement and military power. And... federal judges are appointed for life. Forget contested elections, power-hungry politicians, or any bar association, federal judges cannot be removed from the bench short of egregious, felonious conduct. A federal judge is as close to a god as a democracy dares allow.

> A FEDERAL JUDGE IS AS CLOSE TO A GOD AS A DEMOCRACY DARES ALLOW.

At the time of our lunch, President Reagan and the law and order crowd had convinced Congress that federal judges were not giving criminals enough jail time. They thought the courts were "soft" on crime. So Congress enacted legislation creating mandatory federal sentencing guidelines, eliminating some of the judges' discretionary powers, at least when it came to sentencing. The judge carped openly, between sips of expensive merlot, about those "moron congressmen" and their ability to curtail a federal judge's "constitutional prerogative." History has shown the judge's rankling to be on the mark. We now have prisons full of nonviolent marijuana users doing ten years or more under the mandatory sentencing guidelines.

As a gorgeous tray of too-pretty-to-eat desserts was wheeled to the side of our table, the judge announced that no one was going to screw with his plan to exact pain on those "greedy bloodsuckers" that sent our banks down the tubes. (I digress. At the time, the nation was in the throes of a banking industry meltdown and the government was looking for people to blame. They sued the borrowers, the bankers, the lawyers and accountants who worked for the bankers, and anyone else from whom they thought they could recover money. Because the banks were federally insured, most of these cases ended up in front of federal judges.)

The judge relished the thought of the local bigshot real estate developers being forced to give up their Gulfstreams and young trophy wives. As a collection attorney, I interjected that even when rich people seem to lose everything, they never end up living like poor people. They always seemed to hang on to their cash and their lifestyles. The judge pursed his lips, flipped his hand towards the waiter, and in the manner that only a guest certain his subordinate host will be paying the check can do, ordered a generous snifter of brandy rated with enough stars to fill a flag.

As he gently swirled the mahogany colored brandy in his heated snifter, the judge cleared his throat. An untimely interruption here could cost you jail time. I sat up straight. . . and waited. Either he was going to play the mentor and share some valuable tribal secret with me or I was going to get one of those "why in the hell did you choose to be a collection lawyer in the first place?" lectures. He gently set his snifter directly in front of him and cupped both hands around the bowl of the glass. He looked me squarely in the eye and without a trace of emotion in his voice – but with the steely resolve that only a man with the power to sentence someone to death can give – he said evenly, "Bill, if you can find an asset anywhere within my jurisdiction (i.e. the United States), I can seize it. Don't ever forget that." (I didn't.)

With that, he placed his starched white napkin on the table, thanked me for lunch, and excused himself. It may not have been a tribal secret, but it confirmed the worst nightmare of every defendant and lawyer. No matter how carefully you attempted to protect an asset – partnerships, trusts, whatever – if a federal judge can find it, there is a chance you could lose it.

> "BILL, IF YOU CAN FIND AN ASSET ANYWHERE WITHIN MY JURISDICTION (I.E. THE UNITED STATES), I CAN SEIZE IT."

This lunch was a turning point for me. Something clicked. Epiphany, revelation, awakening . . . whatever you want to call it, I realized I was in the wrong business. I was pounding my way through the courts day after day for a percentage of whatever assets I could recover from a bunch of unwilling, feisty debtors. On the other hand, what would people pay to protect their assets from such a system?

If a federal judge could locate an asset, he could seize it. A rational person would argue that this is illegal, unconstitutional, or at least, immoral. And they would be right. But federal judges are appointed for life; to appeal their decision takes years, and it costs a fortune!

As the 1980s ended, the banking industry was in shambles and dragging down the real estate industry with it. At that time, my practice was limited to doing evictions and collection work for the wealthy owners of apartment complexes and other commercial buildings. Many of these same clients lost their real estate holdings to foreclosure and were preparing to be sued by lenders, partners, and the federal agencies that insured the banks. They implored me to find a safe haven for their cash and other liquid assets.

As all lawyers with a whit of common sense seem to do in their fifteenth year of practice, I was suffering from burnout. A few years ago a poll was taken of all California lawyers. Over 70 percent of those questioned admitted they would quit the practice of

> OVER 70 PERCENT OF THOSE QUESTIONED ADMITTED THEY WOULD QUIT THE PRACTICE OF LAW IN A HEARTBEAT IF THEY COULD AFFORD IT.

law in a heartbeat if they could afford it. You have to figure that half of the remaining 30 percent were fudging, so I figure closer to 85 percent of all California lawyers would quit if they could. They just couldn't bring themselves to admit they'd wasted so much time and money to become a member of a profession that offered so little beyond a steady income.

I, however, took the plunge. After appearing in court for the last time in 1990, I surrendered my license, moved to California, and carved out a career outside the courtroom protecting people's assets.

Recalling the judge's words, I realized that any asset protection plan needed to include two elements to succeed:

1. Privacy. To avoid seizure, an asset must be difficult or impossible to find.

2. A safe haven. Some assets would have to be placed beyond the grasp of my federal judge friend. That would mean outside the United States. Let's consider the privacy issue first.

CHAPTER 2
PROTECTING YOUR PRIVACY

Camouflaging your assets is the first step in implementing any asset protection plan. Remember, if a federal judge can find an asset, he can seize it. Conversely, what he can't find, or doesn't know about, he can't touch. Although I enjoy advertising bulletproof asset protection, the prescription for making an asset bulletproof is first to make it invisible.

One of my long-standing asset protection clients is a wonderful guy I'll call Gino. Gino made his money in the "adults only" business. He's close to seventy years old (doesn't look it) and lives in a beautiful, but modest, home overlooking the ocean in Santa Barbara,

> THE PRESCRIPTION FOR MAKING AN ASSET BULLETPROOF IS FIRST TO MAKE IT INVISIBLE.

California. The house is tastefully appointed and stuffed with mementos Gino has collected during his extensive travels. He rents the home from a Bahamian corporation and sends his monthly rent payments to the offshore bank account of the landlord company. He drives a leased Lexus (not a new one) and routinely eats lunch at Brophy's restaurant in the marina (cioppino, no cheese) where he always pays with cash. His favorite activity is golf. He carries a respectable sixteen handicap and hates slow play. So, he plays anytime he wants as a guest of a corporate member of a private country club. I'm not sure if he has a checking account, but he always has 'two inches' of cash in his left pocket. See, Gino loves to play gin rummy at a buck a point with anyone foolish enough to think he might be an absentminded old man. He files all of his tax returns religiously and tips service people generously. Everyone knows his first name. If you won a lawsuit against Gino, you might be able to seize his used golf clubs, but that's about it. He carries an offshore debit card in a corporate name that works in any ATM machine. Financially speaking, Gino is invisible. Psychologically speaking, Gino never worries about lawyers, or the IRS, or much of anything else for that matter. He's lived this way since I met him in 1990.

Personal privacy, especially in financial matters, although constitutionally protected, is routinely violated by collection agencies, private investigators, and the government, especially with the advent of the Internet. As a former collection/eviction attorney, I routinely accessed the following records to learn about a debtor's assets and personal life:

1   Voter registration records

2.   Workers' compensation information

3.   Sheriff and county prosecutor records

4.   Real estate recording records

5.   Fictitious business name records

6.   Professional licensing boards

7.   Corporate registration records

8.   Marriage license records

9.   Property tax records

10. Utility and credit card bills

11. Litigation, divorce, and bankruptcy files

12. Probate records

13. Medical records

14. Telephone records

If your name appears in any one of these records, it could be linked to the remainder of the records. It should also be noted that we were able to get to all this information before the advent of the Internet.

After the Oklahoma City bombing in 1995, President Clinton submitted a bill to Congress making it easier for federal authorities to check your personal records and use electronic surveillance and wiretaps more freely. The government can secretly obtain your financial records without accusing you of any crime under the Patriot Act.

The loss of personal financial privacy can be traced directly back to the 1980s and President Reagan's "war on drugs." Remember the "Just Say No!" campaign spearheaded by first lady Nancy? It was decided that since the DEA couldn't stop the entry of drugs into the country at the borders, maybe the feds could disrupt the drug business by seizing the drug dealers' money. How this policy was somehow going

> THE GOVERNMENT CAN SECRETLY OBTAIN YOUR FINANCIAL RECORDS WITHOUT ACCUSING YOU OF ANY CRIME.

to decrease the demand for drugs was never explained. This development was coupled with the fact that the federal government was forced to take over hundreds of failed banks and savings and loans during this same period. You may remember the now defunct Resolution Trust Corporation, better known as the RTC. This was the federal agency that liquidated hundreds of failed banks.

As a result of this widespread involvement of the federal government into the private banking business, any notion of banking secrecy or even privacy was washed away. Prior to this time, a bank's primary obligation was to protect its customers' privacy and money. But in the 1980s, any bank or financial institution insured by the government (FDIC) became an agent or extension of the federal bureaucracy. The banks shifted their loyalty from their customers to the feds. The government insured their deposits, provided them with liquidity by way of the Federal Reserve, and cleaned up their mess when they engaged in reckless lending. The simple depositor or checking account customer held no such sway. After the S & L crisis of the 1980s and subsequent bailout, the federal government felt they had earned the right to meddle into and more closely regulate the affairs of its member banks.

> ANY NOTION OF BANKING SECRECY OR EVEN PRIVACY WAS WASHED AWAY.

Couple this development with the war on drugs, and you can see how the currency transaction report (CTR), the requirement for banks to report any "suspicious activities" of its customers, and the concept of "structuring" entered the banking lexicon. Suddenly, anyone dealing in cash was assumed to be doing something illegal. Any customer depositing or withdrawing more than $10,000 in cash requires the bank to prepare a CTR to be filed directly with the federal government. Carrying more than $10,000 in cash in or out of the country requires a declaration of same to the U.S. Customs Service. Customs agents routinely seize cash, even amounts less than $10,000, at border entries if they believe the traveler is "suspicious" looking. The hapless traveler's only remedy is to hire an attorney, sue the federal government, and beg to get his money back.

If you deposit $9,000 in cash one day and $2,000 the next, you can be charged with "structuring" your deposit to avoid the CTR requirements. This is a felony.

At the congressional hearings on the abusive activities of the IRS in 1998, a parade of everyday taxpayers testified that the agency had investigated every aspect of their lives to determine if they would make profitable targets for an audit. Everyone claimed to be outraged and Congress promised the IRS would change their ways, but not a single IRS agent was dismissed as a result of the scandal. Arkansas Senator David Pryor (D) responded to the hearings by saying the evidence "confirmed the worst fears about government mismanagement of data concerning private citizens."

> IF YOU DEPOSIT $9,000 IN CASH ONE DAY AND $2,000 THE NEXT, YOU CAN BE CHARGED WITH "STRUCTURING" YOUR DEPOSIT TO AVOID THE CTR REQUIREMENTS. THIS IS A FELONY.

The most recent justification given by the federal government to further limit our right to privacy is the "war on terrorism." The Posse Comitatus Act of 1878 is supposed to protect us against a president using the army to enforce the law against civilians, but in 1996 President Clinton issued a presidential decision directive to authorize military intervention against terrorism on our own soil giving the military the power to do anything necessary to stop any perceived threats from terrorists. It isn't much of a stretch to assume that if any of your financial activities are perceived to be for the benefit of terrorists your accounts will be seized.

President and part-time cigar smoker, Bill Clinton, personally ordered a missile strike on a pharmaceutical plant located near Sudan's capital city on August 20, 1998, the night of Monica Lewinsky's return to the grand jury and just three days after his pathetic "apology" bombed on national TV. He claimed the plant was manufacturing components used to make VX nerve gas and that it was being financed by Osama bin Laden, the crazy, rich Saudi entrepreneur wanted for the deadly attacks on U.S. Embassies in Africa. This all turned out to be another presidential lie, of course (See *Vanity Fair*, March 1999, "Weapons of Mass Distraction" by Christopher Hitchens). Clinton's attack destroyed the plant and killed one person, but Defense Secretary William Cohen eventually was forced to admit that the plant did make medicine. But as Clinton would say, "Let's move on."

The parts of this story that went generally unreported were the activities of the U.S. Treasury Department. The plant was owned by Salah Idris, a Sudanese native now living in Saudi Arabia. Immediately after his plant was wrongfully destroyed, the U.S. Treasury Department's Office of Foreign Assets Control froze $24 million of Mr. Idris's U.S. accounts on the grounds he and his money were linked to terrorism. After six months of foot-dragging by the Treasury Department, Mr. Idris was forced to file suit in U.S. Federal Court on February 20, 1999, to get his money back. His lawyers made it clear that Mr. Idris was being made a scapegoat for an American blunder. By claiming that Idris had terrorist ties, U.S. officials

> THE U.S. TREASURY DEPARTMENT'S OFFICE OF FOREIGN ASSETS CONTROL FROZE $24 MILLION OF MR. IDRIS'S U.S. ACCOUNTS.

claimed justification for the bombing and subsequent freezing of his assets. The Treasury Department clearly violated the law by not laying out beforehand Idris's alleged terrorist links or formally declaring him a terrorist.

A short time later, without any notice to the press, the Treasury Department quietly returned the $24 million to Mr. Idris, in effect admitting the bombing was a gross mistake. However, Treasury Department officials have refused to pay Mr. Idris for the damages to his plant, clinging pathetically to their original allegation that somehow the plant was involved with international terrorism. Mr. Idris was forced to file suit against the Treasury Department in federal court in an attempt to recover his damages.

U.S. officials subsequently admitted that they did not know that Mr. Idris had only purchased the plant four months prior to the bombing, but they claimed the former owners may have had links to Osama bin Laden. In the meantime, many Sudanese people have died because their impoverished country had lost its chief source of medicine.

It should be noted that the word "privacy" never appears anywhere in the Constitution. It's easy to understand why Jefferson and the other framers, living in a predominantly agrarian society in the 1700s, weren't worried about people being left alone.

> IT SHOULD BE NOTED THAT THE WORD "PRIVACY" NEVER APPEARS ANYWHERE IN THE CONSTITUTION.

Privacy only became an issue at the turn of the twentieth century with the advent of urbanization, the telephone, national banking, and the Sixteenth Constitutional Amendment creating the federal income tax.

The primary safeguard for privacy in the Constitution is the Fourth Amendment. It states: "The right of the people to be secure in their persons, houses, papers, and effects, against unreasonable searches and seizures shall not be violated." The eloquent Supreme Court Justice Louis D. Brandeis, a champion of individual freedom, said in 1928 in a dissenting opinion, "The right to be left alone is the most comprehensive of rights and the right most valued by civilized men."

The First Amendment's guarantees of freedom of expression and assembly have been interpreted by the courts to apply to the collection of data on political views and associations. Under the free speech provisions, any person can say or not say anything they choose so long as their actions don't harm or violate the rights of others.

This includes the right to use whatever name or other identifying information a person so chooses. Creating an alternate identity is one of our most neglected freedoms. Everyone has the right to change their name and identity so long as it is not done for criminal purposes. For instance, many movie stars, Whoopie Goldberg, Tom Cruise, and Woody Allen, to name just a few, use a second identity, not their birth names. Voluntarily becoming a "missing person" is not a criminal offense.

The Fair Credit Reporting Act of 1970 prohibits credit bureaus from sharing credit information with anyone but its authorized subscribers. It also gives consumers the right to review their credit records. Consumers are to be notified if their credit is investigated by an insurance company or employer. So far, so good. The privacy provisions implicit in this act lost their teeth, however, with the little known provision stating that credit agencies can share their information with anyone it reasonably believes has a "legitimate business need." Virtually anyone can claim they have a business need to look at your credit, so you can figure any of your personal information at any credit reporting agency is easy pickings for any creditor or investigator.

Congress responded to their constituents' complaints about the lack of privacy and passed the Right to Financial Privacy Act of 1978. It was designed to prohibit the federal government from perusing through bank account records without first alleging some kind of probable cause. But the act specifically excluded state agencies, law enforcement officials, and private employers. This turned out be to be more of a public relations ploy designed to placate angry voters than a meaningful attempt to protect anyone's privacy. A few years ago, the federal legislative counsel for the American Bankers Association stated flatly, "There's not a lot to this act anymore."

In 1987, Robert H. Bork was before Congress as a U.S. Supreme Court nominee. Remember him – the brilliant intellectual with the not-made-for-TV facial hair? Senator Kennedy and other liberal senators attacked him mercilessly.

> "THERE'S NOT A LOT TO THIS ACT ANYMORE."

A Washington, D.C. weekly publication, *The City Paper*, went so far as to publish a list of videotapes borrowed by Bork to further discredit him. After defeating his nomination, the Democrats claimed they were outraged by this invasion of privacy and in 1988 passed the Video Privacy Protection Act of 1988. This act is also known as the Bork Bill and it prevents retailers from selling or disclosing video rental records without a customer's permission or a court order. Again, this is a step in the right direction, but there is no such act providing the same protection for medical, insurance, or criminal records.

The Freedom of Information Act

The Freedom of Information Act (FOIA) was enacted by Congress in 1966 declaring that government records should be open to its citizens. Before the act, anyone requesting to see government records had to shoulder the burden of proving they had a right to see the records. The act shifted the burden to the government. You now have the right to access any government record unless the government can prove that the records you're after are "exempt" by law from review.

Even so, the FOIA is limited in scope. It applies only to the records of the executive branch of the federal government, not to those of Congress or the federal courts. It does not apply to any records kept by any state or local government.

The act states there are nine exemptions or reasons an agency may refuse to release its records to the public. The general categories are:

1. Classified materials relating to defense or foreign materials.

2. Geological information relating to oil wells.

3. Any investigatory records gathered for law enforcement purposes.

4. Materials pertaining to internal personnel rules and practices.

5. Trade secrets and other confidential business information.

6. Materials exempted by another statute from disclosure.

7. Some personnel and medical records pertaining to certain persons.

8. Some interagency and intra-agency communications.

9. Matters relating to the supervision of financial institutions.

Under the FOIA, you have the right to request and receive any record in the federal files not covered by one of the exemptions. You can request to see any file compiled by the Federal Bureau of Investigation on Vietnam war protesters during the 1960s or 1970s. You might be amazed at how many files were compiled by the FBI.

Even though the FOIA does not apply to any records held by state or local governments, many states have their own version of the FOIA. You can write the attorney general's office of any state to request state records.

> YOU MIGHT BE AMAZED AT HOW MANY FILES WERE COMPILED BY THE FBI.

Many private firms and companies routinely submit reports and other information to specific federal agencies as may be required by law. This is often the case if the company wants to bid on federal contracts, receive a subsidy, or obtain a license. Although the FOIA does not require a private firm to release any information or records to you, many times the federal agency receiving the information from the private firm will release the information to you on an FOIA request.

Each FOIA request must be made to the appropriate federal agency. The U.S. Government Manual is the official handbook of the federal government. It describes the specific programs within each federal agency and lists the persons to contact with their mailing addresses. This manual is available at most public libraries or on the Internet.

By law, federal agencies are required to respond to your FOIA request for records or information within ten business days from receipt. If the agency needs additional time, they must notify you and they can only extend the deadline by up to ten more working days.

If your request for information is denied, you have the right to appeal. Usually within thirty to forty-five days after you receive your denial letter, you can appeal by asking the agency to reconsider its decision. You ought to give specific reasons to support your appeal. The agency has twenty business days to respond to your appeal letter. If they continue to deny your request, you have the right to file a complaint in your local U.S. District Court and ask for relief. If you prove your case, the judge can even require the government to pay your attorney's fees and court costs.

The Privacy Act

The Privacy Act was passed by Congress in 1974 in an attempt to limit the amount of information the government can collect on its citizens. The act provides for two basic rights: (1) It gives you the right to see the files collected on you by the government, and (2) it gives you the right to sue the government if it reveals your files to others without your permission or knowledge.

The first right may have some practical value to the extent you can gauge if you're the target of an investigation depending on how thick the government file is on you. The second right is utterly meaningless. No one can afford to wage a legal battle against the federal government.

Ongoing Identification Programs

Currently, we all use Personal Identification Numbers (PIN) to access our credit cards, but the banking community is working on tighter controls by using newer identification methods.

The hand-scan machine has already been developed. You place your hand on a glass plate and the machine memorizes every mark and crease on your palm. Your palm print becomes your identification code and eventually could replace all credit cards. The machine can "read" your right hand and link it with an assigned number. I had the opportunity to see this machine in action at a recent trade show in Las Vegas. As we entered the convention center, we placed our right palms on the hand-scan machine which was connected to the exhibit booths. If an exhibitor was selling a product and you wanted them to send you additional information, you scanned your hand at the booth causing your business card to be deposited in the exhibitor's computer database.

> THE MACHINE CAN "READ" YOUR RIGHT HAND AND LINK IT WITH AN ASSIGNED NUMBER.

Several multipurpose computerized ID cards have already been developed. Singapore is a rigidly controlled island nation of three million people and is widely recognized as the banking center for the Orient. Although they claim to be a free democracy, the government has decided it's necessary to keep track of all its citizens to maintain efficiency. Every citizen of Singapore over the age of fifteen carries a computerized ID card which is tied into a computerized data bank that holds every shred of personal information on each of its citizens from a police record to a school loan. (Wouldn't the IRS love to get a hold of this system?)

A number of congressmen have proposed a national ID card allowing us to do away with cash, bills, and coins. When Hillary Clinton single-handedly tried to nationalize the health care system in 1992, she proudly held up a national ID card that would be assigned to every citizen. Fortunately, a federal judge struck that program down. In every session of Congress the idea of a "cashless" society is floated around with the claim that it would make life "easier" for everyone. The goal, of course, would be to monitor every single financial transaction as to its origin and destination. It's not much of a stretch to envision the day when every paycheck is sent directly to Washington allowing the bureaucrats to remove any withholding, income, or other taxes owed with the net balance being sent to the taxpayer.

> A NUMBER OF CONGRESSMEN HAVE PROPOSED A NATIONAL ID CARD ALLOWING US TO DO AWAY WITH CASH, BILLS, AND COINS.

One of the most recent systems designed to collect information and invade your privacy is being assembled by Image Data, LLC of Nashua, New Hampshire. With funding of $1.46 million from no less a snoop than the Secret Service, this private company is assembling a national data bank of driver's license photos. They claim the only use for the data bank would be to combat check fraud and other crimes involving the misuse of personal information. But as Marc Rotenberg, director of the

Electronic Privacy Information Center in Washington said, "This is a high-tech wolf in sheep's clothing. There's a lot more going on here than check verification." At this time, only a few states have agreed to sell their driver's license photos to Image Data, but stay tuned. Image Data calls its system TrueID. When fully operational, the company would send photo images from its data bank to merchants so they can check the identification of customers paying with checks. It's already being test marketed in South Carolina.

Criminal Justice Information

Our criminal justice information system offers the greatest potential to damage people with the information they collect and their ability to allow access to the data.

The FBI alone keeps three sets of records:

1. Investigative files

2. Identification records

3. Those kept by the National Crime Information Center (NCIC)

Investigative files contain the information on cases where the FBI has jurisdiction. Anytime anyone is arrested for anything from a speeding ticket to murder, all of the information is forwarded to the FBI identification records. Since 1973, any person can request a copy of his own identification record from the FBI.

The last category of files kept by the FBI is the NCIC. These track and record an index of stolen property, fugitives, and all criminal histories. If you have ever been pulled over by a highway patrolman, you may have seen the NCIC in action. Before the patrolman leaves his car, you'll see him giving your license plates to the NCIC to see if your car has been stolen.

No one will dispute the need to keep records of criminals, but the abuses come to the fore when a person has an arrest on his record with no conviction. For instance, if you're arrested for drunk driving, but later acquitted at trial, the arrest will not automatically be erased. You must request that the arrest be removed or it could come to haunt you when you apply for a job. After a certain time period, usually three years, many states allow you to seal your criminal record, including all arrests and convictions. In this event, you can answer, under oath, that you have no criminal record and if anyone tries to check they will find nothing.

> THE LAST CATEGORY OF FILES KEPT BY THE FBI IS THE NCIC.

The Internet — Knowing You All Too Well

The Internet is a terrific tool for information and commerce, but its ability to invade our privacy is unlimited and growing every day. Internet commerce has become one of the greatest threats to personal privacy. The World Wide Web has evolved into a marketplace, and in the process transformed privacy from a right to a commodity. High-speed networking and powerful database technologies have made it possible for businesses to amass quickly, and at low cost, a wealth of personal information on over 200 million Americans.

You want to know if a potential business partner has a history of bad credit, lawsuits, or fraud? There are hundreds of investigative sites that will help you. You want to review the executive travel records of your competitor to figure out where they're going and with whom they're meeting? Web companies specialize in "competitive intelligence" and can find this information on their databases.

Accidental breaches of security are common. In August of 1997, the big credit bureau Esperian (formerly TRW) began offering on-line delivery of credit reports, but shut down the service two days later due to a computer glitch. Seven out of 106 first-day applicants received someone else's report.

Deliberate breaches of privacy are more sinister. Identity theft is a disturbing example. Someone obtains basic personal information about you from an on-line data warehouse. Then the person proceeds to impersonate you using your name, credit cards, credit history, medical records, and financial information. Approximately 85 percent of all Web sites collect some personal information from visitors.

> **ACCIDENTAL BREACHES OF SECURITY ARE COMMON.**

Marketing priorities place an ever greater strain on privacy. The Internet not only collects and collates data, it creates new kinds of information. For example, "clickstream" monitoring involves a page-by-page tracking of people as they peruse the Web. Your clickstream reveals your interests and tastes with frightening precision. This information allows merchants to identify the products you are most likely to buy.

On the other hand, Web merchants need to have customer authentication to make sure you are who you say you are. With this in mind, they request all kinds of personal information to make sure the credit card you're using belongs to you. . . and they must

> THE INTERNET NOT ONLY COLLECTS AND COLLATES DATA, IT CREATES NEW KINDS OF INFORMATION.

determine you are you! For this reason, our company increasingly gets requests to help people create a legal second identity; one for regular life and a second for use on the Internet.

Justice Louis Brandeis defined privacy as "the right to be let alone," but in the Internet world this seems almost anachronistic. Arthur Bushkin, CEO of Pace Financial Network, said it best, "The Internet is not just a change in scale or speed, it's a qualitative change. A car is not just a faster stagecoach. Data collection before the network computer was like the stagecoach; data collection in the Internet age is like the car. This is a new problem, not just more of the old one."

The tools available to any lawyer or private investigator in searching for your assets are formidable. If you are at risk from a potential lawsuit, a divorce, or a government agency, the first question will be, "Where are your assets?" There are only two responses to this question and the first one goes something like this:

"I have assets but you can't get them. See, I hired a building full of brutally expensive, silk-stocking lawyers who have assured me that my assets are safely beyond the reach of any of my creditors. I have trusts for the benefits of my kids, a Family Limited Partnership in which I have no control, my house is in my wife's name, and the rest of my assets are protected by a corporation of which I am the president."

Remember my friend, the federal judge? I would not want to recite this response in his court, especially after he'd had a two-brandy lunch. Once your assets are found, you've got to assume he'll use his power as only a man in full can do. Oh, sure, your expensive lawyers will delay their tee time long enough to tell you, "Don't worry, we'll win on appeal." In the meantime, all of your assets are frozen, pending the outcome of the appeal, and don't forget to send $10,000 to your lawyer "to get things started."

The second possible response to the question on the location of your assets goes like this: "I don't have any assets."

> **"I DON'T HAVE ANY ASSETS."**

This is the response I prefer. Short, clean, and direct. Like a perfect murder, the questioner may have a dead body, but in no way is it connected to you.

The first step to privacy and making your assets invisible is the use of a Nevada corporation. Or a series of them. First, let's take a quick look at how a corporation works.

CHAPTER 3
WHAT IS A CORPORATION

Let's review the mechanics of a corporation before we discuss how it can provide privacy. Most people think of a Fortune 500 company like Coca-Cola, IBM, or Microsoft when they think of a corporation. And they're not wrong, but the vast majority of corporations are owned by people with small businesses. Most of the large companies are publicly traded companies with their stock listed on one of the stock exchanges, but most corporations are privately held with fewer than ten shareholders.

If you look in a law dictionary, a corporation is defined as follows:

> *"An artificial person or legal entity created by or under authority of the laws of a state or nation, composed, in some instances, of a single person and his successors, being the incumbents of a particular office, but ordinarily consisting of an association of numerous individuals, who subsist as a body politic under a special denomination, which is regarded in law as having a personality and existence distinct from that of its several members, and which is by the same authority, vested with the capacity of continuous succession, irrespective of changes in its membership, either in perpetuity or for a limited term of years, and of acting as a unit or single individual in matters relating to the common purpose of the association within the scope of the powers and authorities conferred upon such bodies by law."*

The shareholders of a corporation are its owners. They elect the directors of the company to manage the overall direction and policy of the corporate business. They can meet whenever they choose, but in most cases at least once a year. The directors hire the officers to handle the day-to-day operations of the business. The officers hire employees, market the company's goods and/or services, and try to make it profitable. Each corporation has a registered agent to accept service of process in the event the company is named in a lawsuit. Each year the company provides the secretary of state or other designated office in the state where it was incorporated with a list of officers, directors, the name of the registered agent, and in some states, the names of the shareholders.

> THE SHAREHOLDERS OF A CORPORATION ARE ITS OWNERS.

A corporation is a separate and legal "person" in the eyes of the law. The corporation is distinct and different from its directors, officers, members, or shareholders. A corporation can only take action through its officers, directors, members, or agents. As an artificial person, a corporation has its own set of rights, duties, and liabilities not unlike a natural person. The activities of the corporation are recorded in the corporate minute book. When a corporation is formed, you receive a corporate charter which operates like a corporate birth certificate. Natural persons are issued a social security

> A CORPORATION IS A SEPARATE AND LEGAL "PERSON" IN THE EYES OF THE LAW.

number by the government. A corporation is issued an employer identification number (EIN) for identification purposes. A corporation must file tax returns. It can be charged with a crime. And it can be a party to a lawsuit.

What is Stock?

A new corporation is capitalized by the issuance of stock. Stock represents ownership in a corporation. Each state has its own rules as to what can be tendered as payment for stock. In Nevada, a corporation may issue shares in consideration of any tangible or intangible asset. Assets tendered for stock may include cash, services, property, promissory notes, contracts to perform services, or any other security. Very few other states allow such a broad range of assets to be tendered as payment for the issuance of stock.

Intangible assets, such as marketing advice, general legal services, or financial consulting, may be hard to evaluate. In Nevada, the directors have absolute discretion in setting the value of these services allowing a new corporation to get started quickly with a nominal amount of cash. Many companies are started with the "sweat equity" of its founders. These are the people who have devoted their time and energy to developing a product or service that is the centerpiece of the

> IN NEVADA, A NEW CORPORATION CAN GET STARTED QUICKLY WITH A NOMINAL AMOUNT OF CASH.

business and corporation. They can be issued stock for the work they have performed to get the business rolling.

Admittedly, this kind of equity may not convince a bank to loan money to the corporation, but it allows its founders the flexibility to at least get their business off the ground.

A good example of new companies founded with sweat equity are some of the Internet retailers. A Web site is designed on a shoestring budget to sell a certain product. If the Web site is a success, the founders can easily sell some of the equity in their company for cash to further expand the business of the company. In the best case scenario, Wall Street gets interested and offers the newly minted entrepreneurs a chance to sell some of the corporate stock to the public via a public offering making the founders rich people overnight.

What Are Shareholders?

Shareholders or stockholders are the people who own stock in a corporation. Nevada specifically does not place a time period as to when stock shall be issued to stockholders, but if stock is never issued an argument can be made that the corporation is not valid. For a corporation to be valid it must have stockholders or owners. If a corporation has no assets or owners, a court may rule there was no intent to act like a corporation allowing a creditor to pierce the corporation and hold the officers and directors personally liable for any corporate obligations.

The only instance where stock is not issued is when a corporation is formed for the sole purpose of creating an aged or shelf corporation. Typically, our office keeps a dozen corporations "on the shelf" that, like a case of good wine, do absolutely nothing except get older. In this case, there is no reason to issue stock until the corporation is going to be used.

Corporate Officials

What Are the Duties of a Corporate President?

The president's duties are spelled out in the bylaws of the company that define the mechanics of the corporation. Generally, any president is responsible for overseeing the actions of all the other officers and employees of the company. The president reports directly to the board of directors and is responsible for executing their orders.

If a company's stock is falling, it's usually the president who's "called on the carpet" at a directors' meeting to take the blame. In fact, many companies' problems can be traced to a lazy board of directors more interested in playing golf than wrestling with the challenges of directing new policy for the company. Anytime a public company has problems, it's the president who's asked to resign as proof to Wall Street that the board is on the ball (no pun intended).

What Does the Corporate Secretary Do?

The secretary is supposed to maintain the corporate minute book and make sure all the formalities are completed to ensure the company remains in good standing. For instance, he records the minutes of any meetings held by the directors, officers, or stockholders, maintains the stock ledger, and is responsible for issuing stock.

In Nevada, one person may occupy all of the officer and director positions, so as a practical matter one person may perform all the duties of all the officers of the company.

> IN NEVADA, ONE PERSON MAY OCCUPY ALL OF THE OFFICER AND DIRECTOR POSITIONS.

What Does the Corporate Treasurer Do?

As the name implies, the treasurer is responsible for maintaining all the financial records and transactions of the company. He will usually make a report at any board of directors meeting to let everyone know the financial health of the company. A good example on a small scale are homeowners' associations. Usually these are small corporations that collect monthly assessments from each of their member homeowners. At the monthly meeting the treasurer will reveal the bank account balance, expenses paid, and the homeowners that are delinquent.

What Does the Corporate Vice President Do?

Large corporations usually have lots of vice presidents. The title of vice president is often given to a valuable employee in order to enhance his ego and self-esteem. This is a lot less expensive than giving him a raise. I've never met a vice president with a clear job description other than he's waiting to become president.

In Nevada, however, we use this position to provide the beneficial owner of a company with control of the corporate finances while protecting his privacy. The list of officers and directors required to be filed with the Nevada secretary of state must include the president, secretary, treasurer, and director(s). There is no mention of a vice president. This means anyone may be a vice president and this fact will never appear in any public record.

When I serve as a nominee officer for a Nevada corporation, I routinely open a corporate bank account for my client in my capacity as president

> THIS MEANS ANYONE MAY BE A VICE PRESIDENT AND THIS FACT WILL NEVER APPEAR IN ANY PUBLIC RECORD.

of the company. After I open the account, some of my clients want to be added as a signer on the account allowing them to execute wire transfers over the phone. As the president of the corporation, I simply make my client a vice president and instruct the bank to give him full authority to act on behalf of the company. Admittedly, my client's name appears as a signer on the account thereby relinquishing some of his anonymity, but his name never appears with the secretary of state or on any public record. In this scenario, I usually continue to sign all the checks to maintain my client's anonymity, but my client will have the authority to execute wire transfers, which can be completed over the phone with a password, or, with some banks, clients can make the transfer on the Internet.

What Does the Board of Directors Do?

In Nevada, the board may consist of one person and that person may also occupy all of the officer positions as well. The board is elected by the stockholder(s). The board hires and fires the officers. The only requirement for an officer or director is that he be a natural person, not another corporation trust, etc., and be at least eighteen years old. He does not need to be a resident of Nevada or a citizen of the United States.

> THE BOARD IS ELECTED BY THE STOCKHOLDER(S).

By law, the directors are to act in the best interest of the corporation. It is unlawful for them to use their positions for personal gain. These are the cases you read about where the director steers lucrative corporate contracts to his best buddy and forgets to tell the corporation of this relationship. Then the buddy screws up the contract, reveals he was giving kickbacks to his "best buddy" director, putting both of them in a position to be sued or indicted.

In large corporations, serving as a director is considered a plum job that helps make the annual report look good to the stockholders. That's why ex-presidents, former generals, and ex-cabinet members land on the boards of the big companies. Some of them actually contribute to the business expertise necessary to operate the company, while others help former White House interns find employment. Go figure.

What Is the Resident or Registered Agent?

The words resident and registered are interchangeable. Some states use one name, some use the other. In Nevada, each corporation must maintain a registered agent for the corporation in a registered office within the state. A registered agent may be a natural person over eighteen years of age or another corporation. The registered office may not be a mailbox or post office box, it must have an actual street address.

You'll see advertisements offering registered agent services in Nevada and other states. Be careful and check the state requirements before signing up. Many offices are nothing more than mail drops with a local phone number automatically forwarded to the actual residence of the person running the ad. In Los Angeles you'll find wannabe movie producers with impressive corporate names, Wilshire Boulevard addresses, and a Beverly Hills phone number that rings through to a basement apartment in Rancho Cucamonga.

The primary purpose for a registered agent is to maintain a continuous corporate presence in the state of incorporation. Specifically, it provides for a physical address for any legal papers to be delivered in the event the corporation is involved in any litigation or needs to receive a verifiable notice of any kind.

In Nevada, the registered agent must keep a copy of the articles of incorporation, a copy of the corporate bylaws, and the stock ledger of the company or a statement that provides the name and address of the actual custodian of the stock ledger. The stock ledger recites the issuance of all stock certificates and to whom they are issued. Therefore, when my clients demand absolute secrecy, I arrange for the stock ledger to be held outside of the country by a foreigner immune from the effect of any U.S. court subpoena. All we are required to keep in our Las Vegas office is the statement giving the name and address of the offshore person charged with keeping custody of the ledger. Further, we make sure only bearer shares are issued giving our clients bulletproof asset protection.

> THE STOCK LEDGER RECITES THE ISSUANCE OF ALL STOCK CERTIFICATES AND TO WHOM.

What Paperwork Is Necessary to Form and Maintain a Corporation?

As someone in the business of forming Nevada and offshore corporations, I suppose I should make the job of forming and maintaining a corporation sound like a horribly difficult task reserved only for a legal wonk. The truth? Not really. Once a corporation is formed it can be maintained relatively simply and inexpensively.

In most states, to form a corporation all you need to do is prepare and file the articles of incorporation. To maintain a corporation properly to insure it remains in good standing requires the preparation and updating of the following documents:

1. A valid corporation should have a set of signed bylaws that defines the mechanics or internal procedures to operate the company. The bylaws

should be considered a contract between the stockholders and the directors and officers.

As a collection attorney, I was able to convince a few judges to pierce a corporation and hold the officers personally liable for a corporate debt when they were unable to produce an organized minute book with a set of signed bylaws. Legally speaking, a corporation can exist without bylaws, but if there are no bylaws it can be combined with other evidence to convince a judge the business never intended to act like a corporation, giving the judge an opening to pierce the corporate veil.

Bylaws are drafted by the directors and adopted by the shareholders. In Nevada, neither the original bylaws nor any subsequent amendments are required to be filed with the secretary of state. Your bylaws should provide for the following items:

> IN NEVADA, NEITHER THE ORIGINAL BYLAWS NOR ANY SUBSEQUENT AMENDMENTS ARE REQUIRED TO BE FILED WITH THE SECRETARY OF STATE.

a. Specify the date and time of any annual directors and shareholders meetings.

b. Define a voting quorum of shareholders. It could be 51 percent or 67 percent, whatever you decide.

c. Provide for the use of proxies.

d. Specify the number, tenure, and qualifications of the directors and what they are to be paid, if anything.

e. Have a procedure for replacing directors when they leave, for firing them, and state how many are needed at a meeting to have a quorum.

f. Have the same procedures listed above for the officers of the company.

g. Describe the share certificates and the procedure for issuing them.

h. Identify the physical location of the corporate offices and the procedure for amending the bylaws.

2. To maintain your corporation in good standing, make sure you actually hold your annual directors and stockholders' meetings and take minutes of the meetings. Again, if you fail to keep up with these corporate formalities, even with a one person corporation, it provides an attorney with the argument that the corporation never operated like one.

Without minutes of your meetings, a judge or IRS agent can disallow corporate actions such as executive compensation, bonuses, retirement plans, and dividend disbursements. The minutes of any meeting should show that the meeting was properly called, that everyone received proper notice in accordance with the bylaws, or that the notice requirements were waived, and briefly describe what was said. The time, date, and location of the meeting should be noted. The minutes should be signed by the corporate secretary and placed in the minute book. Especially with one person corporations, these formalities are critical to proving the corporation operated independently and separately from the person running and owning the company.

3. Make sure you file the annual list of officers and directors as required by law with the appropriate filing fee. In Nevada, the secretary of state automatically sends the list each year to the registered agent for the corporation.

> **MAKE SURE YOU FILE THE ANNUAL LIST OF OFFICERS AND DIRECTORS**

4. Don't commingle personal and corporate funds. This is the area utilized most often by collection attorneys to pierce a corporation. As an example, on one occasion, I sued a corporation for bouncing a check. The check was for $740, but the applicable statute provided for a penalty of three times the amount of the check plus

> **DON'T COMMINGLE PERSONAL AND CORPORATE FUNDS.**

attorneys fees and court costs resulting in a judgment close to $3,000.

The owner of the corporation closed the business, zeroed out the corporate bank account, and told the judgment creditors to take a hike, which most of them did. In this case, however, my client was a wealthy doctor. . . and he was pissed. He authorized me to hire a private investigator to contact customers of the defunct corporation and examine the depository information on the back of the checks to determine where they had been deposited. Sure enough, some of the checks payable to the company had been deposited directly into the owner's personal account. Making it more interesting, some of the checks were deposited into Mr. Married Man Owner's girlfriend's personal account. After presenting copies of these checks to the debtor's attorney, they paid off our judgment the same day. Commingling funds is prima facie evidence that there was no intent to operate like a corporation.

5. When acting as an officer of a corporation, act like one. If you're acting in your corporate capacity, always sign your name followed by your title. With any corporate contract or document, make sure the word "By:" is to the left of the signature line with the name of the company above, and your name and title below the line. If you sign a corporate contract with just your name, an argument can be made that you personally guaranteed the contract. If your company is dealing with the public, have appropriate business cards and stationary. If your company is based at home, that's fine, but at least have a separate phone line in the company name.

How Do Corporate Resolutions Work?

A corporate resolution is a simple document that memorializes the actions of the directors or stockholders that they have "resolved" to take on behalf of the corporation. A resolution may be part of the minutes of any meeting or they can be drafted separate and apart from a meeting. They should be signed and placed in the minute book in chronological order.

In Nevada, directors or stockholders can pass resolutions anytime so long as they are ratified at the next scheduled meeting. There is no legal language necessary to make a resolution legally binding. I've seen resolutions prepared and signed on the backs of restaurant menus. So long as the necessary parties are present, this is entirely acceptable.

> IN NEVADA, DIRECTORS OR STOCKHOLDERS CAN PASS RESOLUTIONS ANYTIME SO LONG AS THEY ARE RATIFIED AT THE NEXT SCHEDULED MEETING.

A corporate resolution should contain the following:

1. The name of the corporation and the state of incorporation.

2. The name of the person who suggested the resolution, i.e., the president, a director, etc.

3. A notation that a majority of the people necessary to make a decision at this level were present.

4. The text of the resolution. For instance, "It was resolved the above date written that the company would open a checking account at First Bank next Tuesday."

5. The date and signatures of all the individuals who approved the resolution.

How Do Corporate Stock Certificates Work?

Each stockholder in a corporation is entitled to receive a stock certificate, signed and dated by the appropriate officers or agents, that certifies the number of shares the stockholder owns in the corporation. Blank stock certificates can be purchased in bulk from various printing companies. Each certificate should indicate the kind and class of stock represented by each certificate. For instance, most companies only issue common stock and simply won't have any other class of stock.

The stock certificate should also include the following information:

1. The state of incorporation.

2. The number of the stock certificate. Like a new checking account, the first stock may start with any number.

3. The authorized capitalization of the corporation. In Nevada, for instance, each new corporation is authorized to issue 75,000 shares for the standard filing fee. The state will authorize additional shares to be issued upon the payment of additional fees.

4. Any restrictions on the stock should be on the face of the certificate giving notice to any subsequent owner. For instance, a certificate may be issued with the restriction that it can't be sold for a period of one year from the date of the certificate.

Each stock certificate has a stub that is left in the minute book indicating the number of shares issued to that particular person on that date. The backs of certificates are left blank. When the owner chooses to sell or transfer the certificate, he endorses the back causing the certificate to be transferred, redeemed, or cashed.

As owners, the stockholders of a corporation have all the power. If one person or a group of stockholders joins together to form a majority ownership, they can pretty much do anything they want with their corporation.

> **As owners, the stockholders of a corporation have all the power.**

How Does the Corporate Stock Ledger Work?

The stock ledger is the official section of the corporate minute book showing the issuance and transfer of all shares. If a stockholder sells his stock or a certificate is exchanged, the transaction is noted in the stock ledger. Retired certificates are canceled, marked "void," and taped back into the ledger with the certificate's original stub. A stock ledger operates similar to a checking account. Each certificate must be accounted for and the total of outstanding shares must equal the number the board has approved.

Any corporate stock ledger should contain the following information:

1. The names and addresses of any stockholders.

2. The date each of the stockholders became owner of their shares.

3. The number and class of shares stockholders received.

4. The consideration given by the stockholder to receive the shares.

5. The person the shares were transferred from, or, if they came from the company's treasury stock the certificate will be marked "Original Issue" in the stock ledger.

Some states require the registered agent for the company to keep a current copy of the stock ledger at all times. Further, most states require the registered agent to open the stock ledger for inspection by any qualified stockholder or be fined.

As discussed above, Nevada requires only that the registered agent keep a stock ledger statement on hand that provides the name and address of the person who actually has the official stock ledger in their possession. In Nevada, the person responsible for the stock ledger can be located anywhere in the world.

Our office in Nevada serves as the registered agent for hundreds of Nevada corporations, but any client may request that the actual stock ledger be kept by someone living in another country. This means when we receive a subpoena to

> NEVADA REQUIRES ONLY THAT THE REGISTERED AGENT KEEP A STOCK LEDGER STATEMENT ON HAND.

produce the corporate records we can give them the stock ledger statement indicating the stock ledger is in the hands of an attorney in the Bahamas, or wherever. United States subpoenas have no authority in the Bahamas so we are in a position to keep the privacy of the owners of any corporation totally protected.

What about the Corporate Seal or Embosser?

The corporate seal is a legal artifact of ancient English law when a barrister would pour hot wax on the bottom of a document and press his ring into the wax leaving his indelible signature. Most states no longer require a corporate seal, but you won't find many incorporating businesses admitting it. They make money selling the seals and embossers. In Nevada, the state legislature went so far as to write into the corporate statutes that a corporation does not need a corporate seal. As we state in our Web site, "If you want a corporate seal, we'll get you one, but we're selling you mudflaps." None of the banks in Nevada require a seal to open a bank account.

The only instance where a seal may be required is in dealing with some foreign countries. Specifically, the banks in

> IN NEVADA, A CORPORATION DOES NOT NEED A CORPORATE SEAL.

Singapore will ask for a corporate seal that perforates the paper as opposed to just an ink seal, but even then they don't check very closely.

What Are Public Offerings?

An IPO is short for an initial public offering whereby a company sells stock to the public for the first time. Public offerings involve complying with a vast web of state and federal regulations. If you're considering a public offering, you need professional advice to weave your way through the legal maze.

Federally speaking, there is the Securities Act of 1933 and the Securities Exchange Act of 1934. These statutes came about after the "roaring '20s" and the subsequent Crash of 1929. These laws are designed to protect potential investors, by requiring the sellers of stock to provide fair disclosure and information to potential buyers, and to prevent fraudulent securities transactions.

The Securities Act of 1933 requires that any person or issuing corporation attempting any sale of a security should file a registration statement that discloses a wide range of information about the security, the company, and the seller. The act also lists several exemptions from the registration requirement.

As an example, most sales of securities that are made by parties other than the original "issuer" are exempt from any registration. There are a few other exemptions from the registration requirement for the issuers of stock:

1. Intrastate Offerings

If a corporation is conducting business solely in one state where the company was incorporated, and sells its securities only to residents of that state, it is exempt from registration. To sell stock to a nonresident, or, if a resident purchases the stock and then sells it to a nonresident, a violation has been committed. The complications in this area arise over the definition of "resident."

2. Small Offerings

This exemption applies to the dollar value of an offering as opposed to the actual number of investors. Check with the SEC regulations to get the current definition of a small offering.

3. Private Placements

A private placement of stock is exempt from registration. This is the most commonly used exemption by small businesses. A private placement is defined as a sale or solicitation to not more than thirty-five people. Efforts to advertise or actively sell the stock to potential investors are prohibited. The intent in this instance is to sell stock to your friends, relatives, employees of the company, suppliers to the business, or other people personally aware of the activities of the corporation.

> A PRIVATE PLACEMENT OF STOCK IS EXEMPT FROM REGISTRATION.

All federal securities laws and regulations apply to any U.S. corporation in any state. Nevertheless, each state has its own rules regulating the sale of stock. These rules generally center on the concern about taxing any activities of the corporation. Most state regulations, called "blue sky laws," prohibit fraud in public offerings by requiring complete disclosure of the offering through state registration. If a corporation intends to sell stock publicly outside of its home state, the offering must qualify for exemption or comply with all of the various blue sky laws in the states where the offering is to be made.

Nevada corporations are allowed to sell stock to as many as twenty-five stockholders per year without needing any additional authorization from the state to hold a public offering. If there are to be more than twenty-five stockholders, a corporation can routinely file the forms with the secretary of state for an intrastate offering that will allow additional sale of stock, so long as the sale takes place within the boundaries of the state. One of the requirements is the filing of a formal prospectus for the stock offering with the securities division of the secretary of state's office.

Nevada has carefully classified shares of stock as personal property. This means individuals can sell shares on their own, with no regulation, any time they choose.

> NEVADA HAS CAREFULLY CLASSIFIED SHARES OF STOCK AS PERSONAL PROPERTY.

What Kinds of Stock Are There?

The terms "stock" and "shares" are generally synonymous. They both represent an ownership interest in a corporation. The effect of ownership is that each share entitles the owner to a share of the profits of the company and a share of any funds left over, if any, in the event the corporation is dissolved. Ownership of stock is physically represented by stock certificates. A stock certificate is an acknowledgment from the corporation that the holder has an interest in the company's property and/or assets. When you trade with a broker or on the Internet, your purchase is recorded, but in most cases the actual certificate is not delivered to you unless you so request.

The value of a stock certificate is generally not fixed, especially if the stock is traded on the open market. A stock certificate can be exchanged for something of value making it a negotiable instrument. There are ten common varieties of stock:

> A STOCK CERTIFICATE CAN BE EXCHANGED FOR SOMETHING OF VALUE MAKING IT A NEGOTIABLE INSTRUMENT.

1. Authorized Stock

Authorized stock refers to the total number of shares authorized to be issued by the corporation as stated in the articles of incorporation. There is no requirement that all the authorized shares ever actually be issued, but if there is a need to issue more shares than are authorized the articles must be amended accordingly.

2. Common Stock

Common stock is used by a corporation with only one class of stock. Common stock is sold to raise capital for the operation of the corporation. Common stockholders are entitled to their prorated share of any annual dividends based on the number of shares they own. Common stock may be divided into different classes. The most common classes of stock are "voting" shares and "nonvoting" shares. Usually, stock certificates reflect the class of stock by stating the class on the face of the certificate: For instance, "Class A Voting Common Capital Stock," or "Class B Nonvoting Common Capital Stock."

3. Preferred Stock

Preferred stock is a class of stock giving the owners a preferred status when dividends are distributed. They receive dividends before any of the common stockholders. Many times the company will give preferred stockholders a specific annual return. For instance, the preferred stockholders may be given a 5 percent annual dividend each year. The company pays this obligation before paying any dividends to any of the common stockholders. Publicly traded companies are careful to pay the preferred shareholders in a timely manner or Wall Street gets nervous, causing a sell off of their common stock and knocking the price down.

Preferred stock can be either "cumulative" or "noncumulative." Cumulative stock means that if one year the company doesn't have the money to pay the preferred stockholders their guaranteed dividend, the guaranteed dividend is added to the next year's dividend. This continues each year until the accumulated dividends are paid. Noncumulative preferred stockholders simply lose their dividend in the year the company doesn't pay them.

4. Treasury Stock

Treasury stock refers to shares issued to individuals and subsequently reacquired by the corporation. Many companies will institute a stock buyback program when they feel the price of their stock is unreasonably low. This also serves as a vote of confidence for the operations of the company. Once the stock is bought back from the public, the shares are held in the corporate treasury where they can remain until the board of directors decides otherwise. The stock can be retired or reissued and sold again. In no event, however, do the shares of treasury stock give the company its own voting rights.

5. Deferred Stock

Deferred stock refers to a class of stock that receives no dividends until after dividend payments have been made to other, more senior classes of stock. As an example, common stock is deferred stock if preferred stock has been issued. Nevada allows for the creation of an unlimited number of stock classes.

6. "Participating" Preferred Stock

This is a special form of preferred stock entitling the owners to participate in any earnings the common stockholders are to receive in addition to the guaranteed dividend already paid to the preferred stockholders.

7. Restricted Stock

This refers to any stock issued by the company that can't be immediately sold or transferred. For instance, when a company sells some of its stock to the public by way of an initial public offering (IPO), the insiders of the company are restricted from selling any of their stock for one year. Another common restriction is a first right of refusal. This allows the company a chance to buy back certain shares of stock bearing this restriction before anyone else.

8. Assessable Stock

This is a stock you don't see very often because it flies in the face of one of the advantages of owning stock in the first place: limited liability. With assessable stock, a corporation retains the right to assess or bill its stockholders if it needs additional cash. In most cases, if the corporation needs extra cash, it will simply sell additional shares of stock rather than bill its existing shareholders.

9. Redeemable Stock

In this case the corporation retains the option to purchase stock back from its stockholders. The buyback price is usually set in advance and sometimes there is a limited time period during which the redemption may take place.

10. Convertible Stock

This allows the corporation or the stockholder to convert or change the stock from one class to another. The best example is where preferred stockholders have the right to convert their stock to common stock, allowing them to take advantage of a rising price in the common stock.

Now you've got a feel for the different kinds of corporate ownership. Let's look at the different types of corporations.

The C Corporation and the S Corporation

In Nevada, the standard corporation is called a C corporation. It is required to pay federal income taxes and if it pays dividends to its stockholders, they are required to pay taxes on their dividends. This is where all the hoopla comes from about the fear of "double taxation" when it comes to owning a corporation. Anyone who allows their business to be doubly taxed is doubly stupid.

> IN NEVADA, THE STANDARD CORPORATION IS CALLED A C CORPORATION.

The S corporation refers to Subchapter S of the Internal Revenue Code that qualifies a C corporation to be taxed differently. The S status of a corporation is not automatic. The corporation must file Form 2553 with the IRS requesting the corporation be given S status for tax purposes. Once the C corporation is qualified by the IRS as an S Corporation, the corporate structure becomes a hybrid structure offering limited liability for its corporate stockholders but the corporation is no longer a taxable entity. Any income the corporation generates, whether distributed or not, is transferred directly to the stockholders who then pay taxes on this income at the appropriate personal income tax rate. Voila! The double taxation ogre is gone. The profits are taxed only once at the shareholder level. The corporation pays no taxes (except on certain types of capital gains). So far, so good. The corporation, in essence, is taxed like a partnership with the stockholders being taxed like partners.

Disgruntled owners of C corporations, however, struck back. To prevent double taxation, they simply didn't distribute their profits. Naturally, Congress got nervous and passed section 531 et seq. of the IRS which penalizes a corporation that accumulates profits "for the purpose of avoiding the income tax with respect to its shareholders." The law states that a corporation may only accumulate profits which are reasonably necessary for business.

Owners of C corporations counterpunched. (Who does Congress work for, anyway?) To avoid the penalty for the accumulation of profits, closely held corporations discharged their profits in the form of nontaxable fringe benefits such as meals, health insurance, life insurance, company cars, gasoline, parking, and every kind of business entertainment they could get away with. Congress immediately tried to limit corporate deductions and certain expense items, but the battle continues.

S corporations also have no corporate tax on the sale of corporate assets, or upon the winding up and sale of the assets of the

> YOU CAN CONVERT A C CORPORATION INTO AN S CORPORATION BY FILING IRS FORM 2553, WHICH MUST BE SIGNED BY EACH STOCKHOLDER.

company. With an S corporation, any losses generated by the company can be taken directly by its shareholders. S corporations are not subject to any accumulated earnings penalties or the personal holding company tax, if any. You can convert a C corporation into an S corporation by filing IRS form 2553, which must be signed by each stockholder. This form has to be mailed to the Internal Revenue Service within 75 days of starting business.

Existing C corporations can elect S status within 75 days of the start of any corporate tax year.

From strictly a tax perspective, there is no question that an S corporation sounds like a great deal. But now, the bad news:

1. Stockholders in an S corporation are subject to tax on the income of the corporation whether they receive a distribution of profits or not.

2. If the corporation must retain some of its income for whatever reason, the individual shareholders must pay any taxes due out of their own pockets.

3. An S corporation may not have more than 35 stockholders. Further, nonresident aliens, other corporations, and partnerships may not hold S stock.

4. As for asset protection, an S corporation offers absolutely no privacy. Each shareholder must disclose to the IRS his name, address, number of shares owned, when the shares were acquired, and social security number to take advantage of any of the tax benefits listed above.

Any collection attorney can subpoena a copy of the federal tax return of an S corporation and learn everything he needs to know about its owners. For asset protection, an S corporation simply won't work.

> AS FOR ASSET PROTECTION, AN S CORPORATION OFFERS ABSOLUTELY NO PRIVACY.

An S Corporation May Be Useful If:

1. The new corporation anticipates there will be large losses at the outset.

2. The business does not need multiple classes of stock, never intends to go public, and wishes to avoid the alternative minimum tax.

3. The stockholders have no desire to protect their identity for asset protection purposes.

·What Is a Personal Service Corporation?

A personal service corporation is designed specifically for small service businesses such as lawyers, architects, accountants, etc. These corporations use a calendar year with a limit of $150,000 on accumulated earnings. The current tax rate for a personal service corporation is the flat corporate rate of 35 percent, instead of the graduated rate that currently starts at 15 percent.

To qualify as a personal service corporation, 95 percent of the employees' time must be spent working in one of several specified fields. In addition to the jobs listed above, this group includes actors, musicians, doctors, nurses, dentists, veterinarians, and consultants paid for their advice and counsel (as opposed to commissions).

What Is a Holding Company?

If any corporation owns or "holds" control of one or more other corporations, it is called a holding company.

The Internal Revenue Service defines "control" of another corporation as consisting of at least 80 percent ownership of its stock. At that point, the corporations are able to combine their income and expenses for filing a consolidated tax return or they can put together a consolidated financial statement to apply for financing. The company being "held" is usually called a subsidiary of the parent holding company.

What Is a Nonprofit Corporation?

A nonprofit corporation is organized for a public or charitable purpose and has been approved by the IRS as a tax exempt corporation. Nonprofit corporations do not issue shares or have any ownership. A nonprofit corporation must have at least five directors or trustees, and upon dissolution must either distribute its assets to the state or federal government or to some other entity qualified by the IRS as exempt.

Personally, I don't think I've ever formed a nonprofit corporation for private use. There are just too many limitations. A corporation formed for profit may engage in any lawful business activity. Nonprofit corporations are required to state a specific purpose that benefits either the public at large, a specific segment of the community, or some membership-based group.

However, occasionally you'll see someone set up a nonprofit corporation for charitable purposes with the intent to realize the applicable tax benefits. As an example, when actor Christopher Reeves broke his neck, a nonprofit corporation was established to raise money to help him pay his medical expenses.

Nonprofit companies may have employees, pay appropriate salaries, and operate like a for profit corporation. In order to claim a nonprofit, tax-exempt status, the corporation must be formed for religious, charitable, scientific, educational, or literary purposes. Only if the corporation has been qualified as a tax-exempt entity can it proceed to solicit tax deductible contributions from donors. Contributions to nonprofit corporations are exempt from federal estate taxation, causing wealthy people to make contributions in their estate plans to qualified nonprofit corporations.

Even though nonprofit corporations are tax-exempt with regard to their specific activities, they may generate income from activities outside their avowed tax-exempt purposes. In this event, this unrelated income is subject to taxation.

The biggest abuses with nonprofit corporations occur in the religious area. Remember Jim and Tammy Bakker? Someone can establish a one-person church, file as a nonprofit corporation, and then get on television and ask for donations. As the late great comedian Sam

> REMEMBER JIM AND TAMMY BAKKER?

Kinison used to point out, "Where does Jesus say in the Bible that a preacher should have a TV show and a private jet?"

Nonprofit corporations enjoy a few specific advantages over regular corporations:

1. Their postal rates are lower on some mailings.

2. They are eligible for many state and federal grants.

3. They usually get reduced advertising rates and any government filing fees are less.

To maintain their tax-exempt status, every nonprofit corporation must comply with the IRS rules:

1. They must operate for religious, charitable, educational, scientific, or literary purposes. When preacher Jimmy Swaggart was caught with his hooker girlfriends, the IRS opened an investigation into his corporation's nonprofit status.

2. A nonprofit corporation may not distribute profits or gains to directors, officers or members. Remember the United Way scandal? It has been estimated that less than ten cents of every dollar contributed ever reaches the intended recipients with many bigtime charities. All the money is eaten up by the "expenses" of operating the charitable organization. The officers are careful not to receive any profits directly, but they're not bashful about buying private jets and throwing outrageous parties called fundraisers.

3. Nonprofit corporations are not supposed to engage in some legislative or political activities as defined by federal law. Specifically, they are not supposed to endorse or denounce any candidate for public office.

4. If a nonprofit corporation goes out of business, it must distribute the remaining assets to another qualified, tax-exempt entity, group, or governmental agency.

What Is a Close Corporation?

A close corporation refers to an entity designed for a small group of investors who act like a partnership, even though they retain corporate liability protection and the other advantages of a corporate structure. A company of this kind is "closed" to any outside investors by restricting ownership in the company and the dissemination of any corporate information.

A close corporation can have a maximum of thirty stockholders and in most cases is prohibited from making any public offerings. All corporate documents and records must clearly indicate that the entity is "a close corporation."

> **A CLOSE CORPORATION ACTS LIKE A PARTNERSHIP.**

In my experience, most close corporations are owned by a group of investors who know each other. A group of family members may form a close corporation to purchase and operate a restaurant. With a close corporation, there are restrictions on the transfer and sale of any stock. If a family owns and operates a restaurant, they might limit the transfer of shares to other family members. In Nevada, stockholders of a close corporation are allowed to "treat the corporation as if it were a partnership or to arrange relations among the stockholders or between the stockholders and the corporation in a way that would be appropriate only among partners."

In a close corporation, the board of directors' powers can be severely limited by a stockholder agreement. Returning to the restaurant scenario, several of my clients use a separate close corporation for each restaurant they open so if one goes broke the others are not affected.

Advantages of Corporations over Sole Proprietorships and Partnerships

1. Limited Liability – In a sole proprietorship or general partnership, the owners' personal assets can be attacked by their business creditors. On the other hand, as owners of a corporation, the shareholders are not personally liable for the debts or the liabilities of the company. Their exposure is limited to their investment in the company's stock.

2. Flexibility – A corporation allows for more opportunities to plan for tax reduction. With the use of pension and profit sharing plans, medical reimbursement plans, and the allocation of salaries and expenses, many corporations can avoid onerous taxation.

> SHAREHOLDERS ARE NOT PERSONALLY LIABLE FOR THE DEBTS OR THE LIABILITIES OF THE COMPANY.

3. Continuity of Ownership – With most businesses, when the owner dies the business closes. With a corporation, there is a set of bylaws that describes with specificity the procedures for replacing an officer or director. Shares of stock are personal property, so if the owner dies, the stock is given to the person designated in the will. In any event, the corporation may continue operating without a glitch.

4. The corporation is separate from its owners. If the corporation has credit problems, it does not affect the shareholders. As for privacy, our company provides nominee officers and directors for our clients' corporations. And Nevada permits bearer shares allowing the owners of the company to maintain total anonymity.

A corporation may be qualified by the IRS as a subchapter S company allowing the profits of the company to pass directly to its shareholders and avoid corporate taxation. A corporation may also be qualified as a nonprofit corporation upon the approval of the IRS and the state where the company is formed.

The Limited Liability Company (LLC)

The newest hybrid kind of corporation is a limited liability company. The LLC was first allowed in the United States in 1977 when Wyoming passed a Limited Liability Company Act. It wasn't until 1988 that the IRS issued a formal opinion on

> THE NEWEST HYBRID KIND OF CORPORATION IS A LIMITED LIABILITY COMPANY.

Wyoming's act concluding that the LLC formed under the act should be classified for federal income tax purposes as a partnership, even though none of the managers or members are personally liable for the obligations or debts of the company. Some of the benefits of an LLC are:

1. Limited Liability – With an LLC, the owners are called members. Just like a regular or C corporation, the liability of the members of an LLC is generally limited to their investment in the LLC.

2. Protection from Creditors – Like a C corporation, the creditors of the LLC cannot attack the personal assets of the members.

3. Taxed Like a Partnership – The tax treatment of an LLC is the primary reason people choose an LLC over a regular C corporation. Like a partnership or a subchapter S corporation, the profits of the company pass directly to its members avoiding double taxation on corporate profits at the corporate level and on the dividends at the shareholder level.

But, to be honest, an LLC is surrounded by a lot of unsubstantiated hype. The tax benefits of an LLC can be duplicated by qualifying a regular C corporation as a subchapter S company. Financial planners and lawyers tout an LLC as the best corporation for asset protection, but the names of its members must be disclosed in the articles of organization destroying any privacy or anonymity for its owners. Bearer shares of a regular C corporation accomplish this goal much more effectively.

Piercing the Corporate Veil

By law, a corporation is designed to protect your personal assets from the claims of any potential creditors or customers doing business with the company. However, there are instances where the corporate veil can be pierced to hold the individual officers, directors, or shareholders personally liable. Different states have different requirements to pierce a corporation. What follows is a summary of events that may allow a creditor to pierce a corporate veil to seize your personal assets to satisfy the debts of a corporation:

1. Criminal Activity or Fraud – If you use a corporation to commit a crime, most states allow the corporation to be pierced to allow the wrongdoing individuals to be prosecuted. For instance, if the president of a company falsifies a corporate loan application to defraud a bank, the officer who signed the application can be prosecuted. He can't claim that only the corporation should be held liable.

> THERE ARE INSTANCES WHERE THE CORPORATE VEIL CAN BE PIERCED TO HOLD THE INDIVIDUAL OFFICERS, DIRECTORS, OR SHAREHOLDERS PERSONALLY LIABLE.

2. Commingling Funds – When you commingle your personal funds with the corporate funds, a creditor can make the argument that the corporation failed to maintain its "distinct and different identity" allowing your personal assets to be attached.

3. Lack of Corporate Formalities – Most states require a corporation to keep annual shareholder and director meetings and to make timely annual corporate filings. If you fail to meet these

requirements, your corporation may lose its "good standing" status, allowing a creditor to set the corporate structure aside to seize your personal assets.

4. Personal Guarantees – Many officers of corporations are not careful when they sign corporate documents. Absolutely every corporate document should be signed in the following manner: "By: (your name) – President (or whatever your position) of (your corporation name).

    If an officer routinely signs corporate documents with his name only, a creditor may successfully argue that the contract included the individual signer in addition to the corporation. This allows the creditor to go after both the corporate assets and the individual signer's personal assets.

5. Alter Ego – This is the area where judges have the most discretion and are most likely to pierce a corporation to hold the individual officers, directors, and/or shareholders personally liable. And this is where privacy as part of any asset protection plan comes into play.

The concept of the corporation was originally created to protect an individual from personal liability. It was seen as a device to encourage entrepreneurs and investors to open new businesses, develop new products, and test market new ideas without having to risk their personal assets. In other words, states created corporations for the primary purpose of protecting people's assets. As I suggested earlier, creditor's rights groups and the federal government have consistently tried to give the concept of asset protection a negative spin, encouraging judges to pierce a corporation, especially if it's in their own self-interest. And to a significant degree they have succeeded.

As a collection lawyer, I argued successfully many times to have a corporation set aside on the grounds it was the owner's alter ego, formed only to protect the owner's assets. Of course, this is exactly the reason corporations were created in the first place. But a judge making a whopping $6,000 or $7,000 a month many times finds it irresistible to use his power to pierce a corporation and make some millionaire fatcat personally pay a debt owed by his corporation. The trouble isn't with the laws governing corporations, it's with the judges who decide when they can be pierced.

> **STATES CREATED CORPORATIONS FOR THE PRIMARY PURPOSE OF PROTECTING PEOPLE'S ASSETS.**

Which leads us back to my lunch with the federal judge described in chapter one. On their face, corporations provide legal and effective asset protection, but if a judge knows and dislikes the owners of the company – and doesn't like them protecting their assets behind the corporate shield – he can use the alter ego argument and seize anyone's assets. "If I can find an asset, I can seize it."

The corporate structure can still be an effective asset protection tool, but it must be coupled with absolute privacy of ownership or it can be denigrated at the whim of a capricious judge. Increasingly, the courts are taking the position that the art of asset protection is a form of "cheating" or is "unfair." It's easy to understand this judicial sentiment when you realize most judges never achieve any kind of financial success. In the old days, judgeships were filled by successful attorneys who wanted to give something back to the bench and the community after a prosperous career. Nowadays, most judges are attorneys who couldn't make it in the private sector, or they're elected hacks indebted to private interest groups, or just plain lazy folks who want a guaranteed paycheck and the respect that comes with the black robe and being called "your honor." (Puh-leez!)

> "IF I CAN FIND AN ASSET, I CAN SEIZE IT."

They're angry and resentful that with all their brains (and a lot of them are smarter than the rest of us) they aren't rich like a lot of the (to them) riff-raff that appears in their court. Then they're asked to rule whether some high school dropout millionaire with a chain of video poker bars should be allowed to have his personal assets protected by his eleven separate, completely legal, state sanctioned corporations. No law is strong enough anywhere to defeat a judge's pride, power, and prejudice.

You may think I'm crying sour grapes about judges, but in August of 1999 the American Bar Association commissioned a poll on people's opinions of lawyers and judges. To their astonishment (not mine), they found that only 27 percent of those polled thought the best lawyers ended up serving as judges. In other words, you can assume a judge is not concluding a successful legal career, but seeking refuge in a government job to escape his failure or inability to make it in the private sector.

Which leads us back to the fundamental precept of any effective asset protection plan: What a judge can't find, he can't seize. And, when asked about your assets, you want to be able to say, "I don't have any assets," not "I've got assets – but you can't get them."

Summary

That's enough of Corporations 101. For asset protection purposes, you need only understand the mechanics of a corporation and the appurtenant corporate language. To be sure, there are volumes of additional information on the life of a corporation, but for our limited purposes of asset protection and privacy, this thumbnail sketch of corporate operations is more than enough.

> WHAT A JUDGE CAN'T FIND, HE CAN'T SEIZE.

There's only one state in the United States that blends the corporate structure with the privacy and anonymity we need for asset protection.

Let's visit Nevada.

CHAPTER 4

THE ASSET PROTECTION ADVANTAGES OF A NEVADA CORPORATION

No question about it, I enjoy touting Nevada as the best place to incorporate. Unfortunately, most people have only experienced Nevada by way of a three-day weekend in Las Vegas. They simply don't think of Nevada as a place to incorporate or conduct business. The most often asked question

> "WHAT ABOUT
> DELAWARE AND WYOMING?"

I receive at my Asset Protection Seminars is: "Nevada sounds great, but what about Delaware and Wyoming?"

What about Delaware?

All fifty states have statutes allowing the formation of a corporation. Delaware was the first state to actively sell itself as a corporate haven. As a small state with limited resources it was the first state to realize the incorporation business could be a generous source of revenue. Delaware enticed people to incorporate there with the promise of limited government intervention and a unique set of complex statutes tailor-made to handle the complicated disputes associated with publicly traded corporations. The strategy worked. Many of the Fortune 500 companies are incorporated there. Almost a quarter of a million companies are incorporated in Delaware. It still leads the nation as a corporate center for American international corporations, but its lead is shrinking.

There are three principal reasons Delaware has developed a reputation as a favorable state to incorporate:

1. Delaware's Tax Laws – Delaware does not tax corporate activities that take place outside the state.

2. Delaware's Court of Chancery – As one of the original thirteen colonies, Delaware has over two hundred years of legal precedents handed down by this unique court. This court was established solely to have the exclusive jurisdiction over Delaware business disputes relating to corporate operations. It has no juries. That's why proxy fights, takeover disputes, or minority shareholder suits of many large corporations end up in this court. These are complicated cases fraught with enormous financial consequences, so combatants want a sophisticated, experienced court to handle their disputes.

3. Delaware's State Legislature – They view the incorporation business as a cash cow for their state and treat it accordingly. They are constantly updating their corporate statutes to reflect changes in the business climate. From the outset, Delaware has framed its corporate statutes to protect the shareholders of large publicly traded companies. To their credit, they have revised their statutes in response to changes in mergers, acquisitions, hostile takeovers, poison pill defenses to takeovers, and other developments affecting publicly traded companies.

Delaware has successfully established itself as the favorite state for large, publicly traded companies. That's the good news. The bad news is that Delaware's laws are not designed for the small business owner or for the purpose of asset protection.

The state of Nevada has stepped in to meet the demands of small business owners, investors, and nonpublicly traded corporate needs. Most corporations formed in Nevada are owned and operated by their owners or by a handful of people. They don't need the Court of Chancery, they want protection and privacy from outside lawsuits, lawyers, and the IRS.

As a comparison, Delaware generally follows the Model Business Corporation Act adopted by most states. The act limits the liability of corporate directors for monetary damages, but it is far less comprehensive than the Nevada statutes. To be specific, the following list of acts can cause officers and directors to be exposed

> THE STATE OF NEVADA HAS STEPPED IN TO MEET THE DEMANDS OF SMALL BUSINESS OWNERS, INVESTORS, AND NONPUBLICLY TRADED CORPORATE NEEDS.

to personal liability in Delaware, while in Nevada the same officers and directors are given protection from such acts:

1. Omissions or acts not in good faith to the corporation.

2. Violation of a corporate director's duty of loyalty.

3. Undisclosed personal transactions benefiting a director.

4. Acts or omissions that occurred before the date that the statute which provides for indemnification of directors was adopted.

In Nevada any acts by officers are exempt from monetary damages. In Delaware, officers are required to reasonably believe that they are completing their duties in the best interest of the corporation. Nevada makes no such distinction in its statutes. By leaving this requirement out, Nevada has effectively prevented any judicial review of the actions of corporate officers or directors except where bad faith or outright fraud is alleged.

One of the biggest problems for Delaware is its administrative requirements and procedures governing and regulating corporate dealings. At an enormous expense, Microsoft relocated its corporate domicile from Delaware to its home state of Washington to avoid Delaware's corporate bureaucracy and high taxes for doing business within the state.

For instance, all businesses incorporated in the state of Delaware are required to file an Annual Franchise Tax Report and pay the franchise tax, if they have not filed for a dissolution or merger within the calendar year. A minimum filing fee of $30 is required to file the annual report. However, for a large corporation, the franchise tax can go as high as $150,000 depending on the company's gross value. Nevada has no franchise tax or related filing requirement.

Another problem for Delaware corporations is the state corporate income tax. This tax is levied on all

Delaware corporations on revenues generated inside the state. Delaware has had the luxury of serving large wealthy corporations over the years, so they're not attuned to smaller corporations' need to keep annual maintenance costs at an affordable level.

> ANOTHER PROBLEM FOR DELAWARE CORPORATIONS IS THE STATE CORPORATE INCOME TAX.

Nevada has no corporate or personal income tax of any kind.

If you're planning to own a publicly traded corporation subject to complex shareholder

> NEVADA HAS NO CORPORATE OR PERSONAL INCOME TAX OF ANY KIND.

litigation, Delaware may be the place. As for the rest of us, we can leave Delaware to the bigshots.

The other state for incorporation that has piqued people's interest is Wyoming.

What about Wyoming?

Well, first things first. Some of the best fishing for Cutthroat trout is on the Snake River, there's no prettier range of mountains than the Tetons, there's a beautiful blonde in Jackson named Bridgit. . . You get the picture.

Wyoming has adopted the Wyoming Business Corporation Act providing a unique set of rules for people incorporating in their state. Listed below are some of the more salient advantages of incorporating in Wyoming:

1. There is no state corporate income tax.

2. Corporations with fewer than fifty shareholders are not required to have a board of directors.

3. One person may fill all required officer and director positions.

4. There are no franchise taxes or taxes on corporate shares.

5. Corporations with fewer than fifty shareholders are not required to conduct meetings, keep minutes, or maintain paperwork associated with having a board of directors.

6. There is no minimum capital requirement.

7. Any annual fees are calculated on the value of the corporate assets located in Wyoming only, not any other assets located outside the state.

8. The Articles of Incorporation may provide for unlimited stock without stating a par value.

9. There is no requirement for issuance of share certificates.

10. Nominee shareholders are allowed.

11. Stockholder lists are not required by the state.

12. As long as any employee or agent of the corporation is acting within his corporate capacity, there is no personal liability. Piercing the corporate veil is difficult.

Let's take a look at the advantages that lend themselves to an effective asset protection plan. No stockholder lists are required. This provides a good measure of privacy. Corporations are never required to disclose the names on any share certificates. However, Wyoming does not allow bearer shares providing bulletproof anonymity. The state does permit nominee shareholders, allowing the true or beneficial owner a layer of privacy, but what happens when Mr. Nominee receives a subpoena? What if he's asked under oath to identify the beneficial owner? If he lies, he's a perjurer. If he stonewalls and loses his memory, the prosecutor will indict him for obstruction of justice. Only

> WYOMING DOES NOT ALLOW BEARER SHARES PROVIDING BULLETPROOF ANONYMITY.

with bearer shares can a corporate officer or its nominee answer honestly and truthfully, "I have no idea who owns the company." Bearer shares are just like cash and can change hands just as quickly. As a nominee officer for hundreds of Nevada corporations, I've been asked this question many times under oath, and my answer is always the same, "I don't know who the owners of the company are and I can prove it." When we form a corporation and issue bearer shares, I specifically ask my client in writing not to tell me what he intends to do with the share certificates. What I don't know I can't tell anyone.

Wyoming also sets its annual fee for maintaining a corporation based on the number of no par value shares of stock, making it more expensive than those states like Nevada with a flat rate renewal fee.

The Wyoming courts have identified a fair number of instances where they will pierce the corporate veil and hold the officers and/or shareholders personally liable:

1. The failure to segregate funds of separate entities.

2. The commingling of company funds and other assets.

3. The unauthorized diversion of corporate assets.

4. Failure to maintain arms-length transactions.

5. The use of corporate assets for personal use.

6. The absence of any major corporate assets.

7. Failure to adequately capitalize the corporation.

8. The unauthorized issue or subscription of shares.

9. Use of the corporation for illegal or fraudulent transactions.

> THE WYOMING COURTS HAVE IDENTIFIED A FAIR NUMBER OF INSTANCES WHERE THEY WILL PIERCE THE CORPORATE VEIL.

Although this list is not nearly as long as in most states, any collection lawyer looks at this list as a goldmine of opportunities to pierce a corporation. Every opportunity to pierce the corporate veil is like a bull's-eye on a corporation's back. As a collection attorney, anytime I attempted to pierce a corporation I started with the wholly unjustified allegation, "Your honor, this corporation is a sham." And if I could show the debtor was using the company jet to pick up his girlfriend, or that money had suddenly left the corporation for a trust in the debtor's children's names, or that the debtor had routinely "borrowed" money from the company, the judge would start to view the corporation in a negative light and declare it a "sham transaction whose sole purpose was to defraud creditors." At this point the debtor's attorney usually asked the court to adjourn for a few minutes to explore settlement talks.

> BUT FOR ASSET PROTECTION, THE STATE OF NEVADA FAR OUTSHINES ALL THE OTHER STATES.

Wyoming is a good place to incorporate. Actually, it's a great place to incorporate if you consider the Snake River and the Tetons.

But for asset protection, the state of Nevada far outshines all the other states.

Why Is Nevada So Special?

Except for a portion of Lake Tahoe in the northwest corner of the state, Nevada doesn't have a whole lot to offer in terms of pictorial beauty or natural resources. It's primarily an endless expanse of moon-like desert with a few treeless mountains connected by parched arroyos. There's a reason it was selected as a nuclear test site. The effect of detonating a nuke in the desert outside Las Vegas was considered redundant.

The construction of the Hoover Dam in the 1930s brought the first real influx of settlers to the Las Vegas area. This was the first project that brought steady work to southern Nevada, but when the dam was completed people had to devise a new form of commerce to provide jobs. Say hello to gambling, prostitution, 24-hour bars, and the promise of individual freedom.

The Depression held back the development of gambling in the 1930s, but during and after World War II the stage was set for Phase I of the phenomenally successful Las Vegas economy. This was the Bugsy Siegel, Benny Binion, Walter Clark era when Frank and the Ratpack ruled the Strip. Phase II began in 1966 with the construction of Caesars Palace and the idea that people might actually want to stay in Vegas for a few days to enjoy the poolside weather and a restaurant other than a buffet. It was then that people realized that Vegas and gambling were not a passing fad. Phase III began with the opening of the Mirage hotel in 1989. Steve Wynn, the owner of the Mirage, successfully thrust Las Vegas into the international limelight as "the entertainment capital of the world." Siegfried and Roy, the white tigers, the volcano erupting every fifteen minutes – whether you're a gambler or not, the concept worked.

Nevertheless, some Nevadans with foresight were concerned that Vegas and the rest of the state would stumble badly if the gambling bubble ever burst. These concerns were first expressed in 1978 when Atlantic City opened as their first real competitor. As a result, in the 1980s, when the total population of the state was less than a million people, the state legislature began exploring the possibility of becoming the incorporation capital. Having already licensed brothels and permitted gambling, making Nevada a haven for creating corporations seemed downright tame.

So in 1987, and again in 1991, the legislature entirely revised the Nevada corporation code. The new laws make incorporation quick, easy, and affordable. They passed laws giving corporate officers and directors liability protection the likes of which had never been seen. They set out to make Nevada the Corporation Capital of the West and they have succeeded. The secretary of state was given the mandate to make the corporations division a profit center, not just another sleepy state bureaucracy. Nevada is currently forming thousand of corporations a year with annual increases in volume estimated at 20 percent a year.

Initially, entrepreneurs and small business owners were attracted to Nevada's incorporation process, but this quickly grew as outsiders realized Nevada was serious about privacy and liability protection for the corporate owners. Rock stars such as Madonna, Prince, Michael Jackson, and Paul Simon are all reported to have Nevada corporations to protect their assets and take advantage of the fact that Nevada has no corporate or personal income tax. Beyond the legal reasons to incorporate in Nevada, there is an intangible benefit that isn't in any statute. There's a pro-business attitude that starts with the precept that a person's business is his business. Nevada is the only state without a reciprocal agreement with the IRS to exchange tax information.

> ROCK STARS SUCH AS MADONNA, PRINCE, MICHAEL JACKSON, AND PAUL SIMON ARE ALL REPORTED TO HAVE NEVADA CORPORATIONS TO PROTECT THEIR ASSETS.

A Nevada corporation may have a bank account, a stock brokerage account, or any other kind of financial services account. There is no requirement that the corporation ever conduct any kind of ongoing business. It can be entirely passive and merely hold a specific asset.

Some of my clients use a Nevada corporation to trade on the Internet to protect their privacy. One of my clients has a separate corporation for his boat, motorcycle, and recreational vehicle. Another client is an inventor with dozens of patents. Each time he launches a new product he forms a new corporation. This falls under what I call the "submarine theory" of asset protection whereby if you take a hit you want to contain any damage and prevent the whole ship from going down.

Las Vegas has been called the town of "second chances." People who have had a brush with the law, gone bankrupt, gotten divorced, or just been unlucky come to Las Vegas knowing they can start over, because people here don't ask a lot of questions. That's the cornerstone of privacy and the incorporation process reflects these sentiments.

Let's take a detailed look at the specific advantages of incorporating in Nevada:

1. Speed. You can form a Nevada corporation in twenty-four hours. If our office receives a request for a corporation before 2:00 PM, you can have a corporate charter the next day. Our runners visit the secretary of state's office

> YOU CAN FORM A NEVADA CORPORATION IN TWENTY-FOUR HOURS.

everyday. We have clients who fax requests to form new corporations, pay with a credit card, and have a local corporate bank account the next day. We have never met many of our clients. Their privacy is our paramount concern.

2.   One-person corporations are allowed. This means all of the officers and directors may be filled by one and the same person. If our clients want total privacy, they ask me to serve as the nominee and I alone can also fill all of these positions. This allows one person to approve and sign corporate resolutions at any time. If our clients choose to have a nominee they only have to pay one annual fee to fill all of the corporate positions.

3.   No personal income tax. Nevadans don't like government as a general rule, especially when it comes to taxes. The Nevada legislature went so far as to make a state personal income tax unconstitutional. Nevada's gaming and tourist industry supply the tax base for Nevada. If you've ever visited Las Vegas, you're aware that we tax every visitor with

> THE NEVADA LEGISLATURE WENT SO FAR AS TO MAKE A STATE PERSONAL INCOME TAX UNCONSTITUTIONAL.

sales, airport, hotel, taxi, and other direct use taxes.

4.   No state corporate income taxes. The rate of taxation for corporations in the forty-six states that have corporate taxes, ranges from 1 percent to more than 12 percent. Further, most states see corporations as having deep pockets, so they levy

surtaxes, surcharges, and in some cases allow local governments to assess their own corporate taxes. California, as one example, has a state corporate income tax of around 12 percent, Arizona's corporate tax is close to 10 percent, and in Pennsylvania, where John Rockefeller first incorporated, there is an onerous 12.25 percent corporate tax. Even incorporation friendly Delaware has a corporate tax of almost 9 percent.

5. No franchise tax. Admittedly, most states have a relatively nominal franchise tax, but it's one less piece of annual paperwork a Nevada corporation has to deal with each year.

6. No tax on corporate shares. Some states tack on a tax every time one of their corporations issues shares of stock. Nevada not only doesn't tax the issuance of shares, it never asks for any information on shares or ownership.

7. No formal information-sharing agreement with the IRS. Or anyone else for that matter. Check the Nevada secretary of state's Web site at: sos.state.nv.us/ and you can see that only the names and addresses of the corporate officers, directors, and registered agent are listed.

8. Minimal reporting and disclosure requirements. As mentioned above, the only disclosure requirements surround the officers, directors, and registered agent for the corporation. There is never a state requirement to disclose the owners of any shares of stock. As for reporting requirements, once each year a one page annual report form must be filed

with a nominal fee listing the current list of officers and directors. There are no other state required filings of any kind.

9. None of the stockholders, directors, or officers is required to live or hold meetings in Nevada or even be U.S. citizens. Any corporate resolutions or meetings can be held anywhere. Each year we form a significant number of Nevada corporations for Europeans and citizens of Caribbean countries.

10. There is no minimum initial capital requirement to incorporate. A company may commence doing business with no assets or capital.

11. Both Nevada corporate statutes and case law make it very difficult to pierce the corporate veil and hold the officers or owners personally liable. This is part of Nevada's goal to make their state the incorporation capital. Specifically, the law states that the only reason a corporation can be pierced or set aside is because of outright fraud. In other words, you just about have to commit a crime before the courts will consider piercing the corporation.

12. Nevada allows for the issuance of bearer shares providing total anonymity for the owners of the corporation. A bearer share is just like cash; ownership resides with whomever holds the certificate in his hand.

> NEVADA ALLOWS FOR THE ISSUANCE OF BEARER SHARES PROVIDING TOTAL ANONYMITY FOR THE OWNERS OF THE CORPORATION.

Nevada state law offers more ways to protect your privacy as a stockholder than any state in the union. To understand how this works, let's look at the five most common methods of determining the stockholders of a corporation:

1. With any lawsuit, each party has the right to gather facts and documents to support their case. In the law this is called discovery and any request for information will be enforced by the judge presiding over the case. Written interrogatories are questions directed to a person who may have information relevant to the case. More often, in the interest of sizing up a potential witness (and increasing billable hours), attorneys will depose or ask questions of a person face-to-face. The questioning attorney is allowed to ask any question even remotely related to the lawsuit. If the deponent refuses to answer the question he can be held in contempt of court. If he lies, or his memory is unbelievably bad, he can be charged with perjury. As a collection attorney, I would depose a corporate officer or director to learn the names of the shareholders when I suspected the debtor might own shares of stock in a private company. Shares of stock are a personal asset and can be seized and sold.

In Nevada, however, with bearer shares, the identities of the owners of any shares are completely protected. In fact, as a nominee officer for hundreds of Nevada corporations, I have been subpoenaed on numerous occasions by collection attorneys, divorce lawyers, and branches of the federal government in their attempt to learn the actual owners of the corporation that I serve as an officer. Forget the attorney-client privilege or asserting your Fifth Amendment privilege against self-incrimination. A judge can set these aside with a wave of his hand, and if you still refuse to talk, you can end up in jail.

Your best and only true protection from a prying question is to be able to answer honestly and truthfully that you don't have the answer. When I'm asked for the names of the owners of any corporation, I can answer cleanly and quickly that bearer shares were issued and I have no idea who has them. It would be like asking me who has the $100 bill that I spent at the grocery store. I gave it to the checkout girl, but I have no idea what happened to it after that.

> I CAN ANSWER CLEANLY AND QUICKLY THAT BEARER SHARES WERE ISSUED AND I HAVE NO IDEA WHO HAS THEM.

Bearer shares are the key to privacy. You can't disclose what you don't know.

The use of bearer shares has an interesting history. The American Bar Association developed the Model Business Corporation Act outlining a relatively generic set of corporate statutes for all the states to follow. That is why most states have similar corporate codes, even though each state legislature puts its unique spin or stamp on their version of the code.

In Nevada, the state legislature adopted many of the provisions of the model act, but then veered off on their own when it came to the information required on any stock certificate issued by any corporation. The model act never mentions or even refers to issuing share certificates to a bearer.

> BEARER SHARES ARE THE KEY TO PRIVACY. YOU CAN'T DISCLOSE WHAT YOU DON'T KNOW.

The model act stipulates that a stock certificate is required to contain:

1. The name of the issuing corporation and the state under which it is organized.

2. The name of the person to whom the stock is issued.

3. The number and class of shares and the designation of the series, if any, that each certificate represents.

The Nevada Revised Statutes carefully omit part of the language in the model act creating the opportunity to issue shares of a Nevada corporation to the bearer. The applicable statute reads in part: "Every stockholder is entitled to have a certificate signed by officers or agents designated by the corporation for the purpose of certifying the number of shares owned by him in the corporation." In other words, Nevada law only requires two things for a stock certificate to be issued:

1. The name of the corporation, and

2. The number of shares represented by the certificate.

Nevada is the only state that allows the issuance of shares to bearer. State officials won't take an official line on the issue, allowing the statute to speak for itself. It should be noted that if you intend to take your corporation public, the rules of the Securities and

> **Nevada is the only state that allows the issuance of shares to bearer.**

Exchange Commission will be paramount. In this case bearer shares could not be used.

In addition to privacy and asset protection, the use of bearer shares allows for the easy transfer of ownership. For instance, if an automobile is owned by a corporation using bearer shares, you can transfer ownership of the vehicle by handing the share certificate to the new owner.

A bearer share is personal property and is regulated by the laws affecting personal property. Like any personal property it can be bought, sold, stolen, borrowed, lost, duplicated, inherited, or willed.

2. In each state you can call, write, or get on-line with the office of the secretary of state or its equivalent and obtain information on any of the corporations

formed there. Most states require a list of shareholders with their addresses to be kept on file. Some states even require the shareholders to list their capital contribution to the company. Nevada does not collect or require any information on its corporate shareholders.

3. All but four states have a state corporate income tax requiring the filing of an annual return. Many states require a list of shareholders to accompany each return. These records can be subpoenaed at any time revealing all the personal information of the shareholders of record when the last tax return was filed.

4. Many states require the resident agent to keep on file a list of the current shareholders of any corporation. In Nevada the resident agent is required to keep a certified copy of the articles of incorporation, but is never required to keep a list of shareholders or even information as to whether any shares were ever issued. Our office serves as resident agent for hundreds of Nevada corporations and we make it a point never to keep or record any share certificates issued. If our records are subpoenaed, they will see a copy of the articles and nothing more. They could have gotten the same information on the Nevada secretary of state's Web site.

5. A lawyer or government agency may choose to subpoena the corporate minute book containing any corporate resolutions or other related documents. A minute book will usually have a

stock ledger containing all the information regarding the amount, type, and value of stock owned by each shareholder. In Nevada, however, there is no requirement to keep a stock ledger, only a statement identifying where the stock ledger is located, and with bearer shares the prying party will learn nothing about the owners. Even if a stock ledger is

> **THE LEDGER MAY BE KEPT OUTSIDE THE UNITED STATES BEYOND THE REACH OF ANY SUBPOENA.**

kept showing the actual names of the shareholders, the ledger may be kept outside the United States beyond the reach of any subpoena.

Nevada goes even further to protect the privacy of its corporate customers. In 1993, the Nevada Legislature amended their statutes, eliminating the right of any judgment creditor to access a corporation's stock ledger, assuming they can find it in the first place. If a creditor attempts to obtain and use any corporate record for any interest other than a shareholder's, they can be assessed civil and criminal penalties.

Subsection three of the applicable statute reads: "Any stockholder or other person exercising (these rights) who uses or attempts to use information, documents, records or other data obtained from the corporation, for any purpose not related to the stockholder's interest in the corporation as stockholder, is guilty of a misdemeanor."

Anyone who uses corporate information for any purpose other than to have stockholders defend or demonstrate their interest in the corporation faces up to one year in the county jail plus a fine. A nonshareholder of any Nevada corporation has no right or authority to view the stock ledger.

What about the IRS?

Nevada has a long history of asserting its independence from outsiders, including the federal government. With legal prostitution, gambling, and the twenty-four-hour lifestyle that goes with it, Nevadans have always been viewed by the feds as a bunch of pirates, mobsters, or worse. Although most casinos are now owned by publicly traded companies with traditional reporting requirements, there is a huge, underground cash economy the IRS would love to get its hands on. To prove the point, the IRS audits a higher percentage of Nevadans than residents of any other state. The Bugsy Siegel days may be over, but Nevada still resents government intrusion into its unique lifestyle.

In 1991, then Governor Bob Miller specifically refused the IRS's request to use state computers to find tax cheats. He also refused to open up employment, motor vehicle, and other records to the IRS because ". . . there is too great a potential for abuse of people's right to privacy." Miller went on to order Perry Comeaux, Director of the State Department of Taxation at the time, to notify the IRS office in southern Nevada

"I TOLD THEM WE WEREN'T GOING TO DO ANYTHING TO EXPAND ANY COOPERATIVE EFFORT WITH THE INTERNAL REVENUE SERVICE."

that state records will not be shared. Comeaux stated flatly, "I told them we weren't going to do anything to expand any cooperative effort with the Internal Revenue Service." That attitude continues to this day.

Most states routinely share unemployment records, welfare and social services records, workers' compensation records, driver registrations, and even motor vehicle registrations with the IRS. Nevada is the only state that does not comply with IRS requests for information.

As an example, California residents who routinely file individual or corporate state income tax returns will have their financial information checked against their federal return without their knowledge. Many states have agreed to this arrangement because the sharing agreements allow the states to have access to IRS records to verify state personal and business tax returns.

There are also reporting agencies and credit bureaus, such as Dun & Bradstreet, that are permanently linked by computer to the various government offices across the country. They keep track of judgments recorded, bankruptcies filed, even the names of the parties in some lawsuits if the information is available.

Now that we all know that Nevada is anti-IRS, the next question is: What if the IRS forces Nevada to sign an information-sharing agreement? Let's assume the worst and assume an information-sharing agreement is signed. Similar to my testimony concerning corporate owners, Nevada can only give the IRS the information it has: the name and address of the registered agent for the company and the name and address of the officer(s), and director(s) of the corporation all of which are already a matter of public record and posted on the Nevada secretary of state's Web site! An information-sharing agreement with the IRS would have no impact on the privacy of Nevada corporate owners as long as a nominee officer/director and bearer shares are being used.

The other question that comes up at my seminars almost every time is, "OK, but what if the IRS cracks down on Nevada corporations?" There is simply nothing to crack down on. Every Nevada corporation is responsible for filing a federal tax return, regardless of how ownership is held. A Nevada corporation by itself does not reduce or eliminate anyone's federal tax liability, but it does provide its owners with anonymity and asset protection.

> A NEVADA CORPORATION DOES PROVIDE ITS OWNERS WITH ANONYMITY AND ASSET PROTECTION.

Naming the Corporation

The Nevada Corporation Code requires that the name of any new corporation not be "deceptively similar" to any existing corporation name. You can check the list of existing corporations by consulting the Nevada secretary of state's Web site. Listed below are words I discourage clients from using in a corporate name simply because use of the word(s) may require approval from other Nevada state agencies:

accident

appraisers

banco

banking

bonding

casualty

college

engineer, engineering

financial

fire

investment

liability

life

loan

mutual purchasing group

reinsurance

risk

risk retention group

savings

surety

trust

underwriter

university

variable

warranty

You may choose from a variety of words to indicate your business is a corporation. Words such as "corporation," "corp.," "incorporated," "inc.," "limited," and "ltd." are all acceptable. Nevada law does not require you to use any of these words as part of your corporate name, unless the name of the company would sound like the name of a natural person. For instance, a corporation could not be called WS Reed but could be called WS Reed, Ltd.

For a nominal sum you can reserve a corporate name with the secretary of state for a period of ninety days and the reservation may be renewed. If your corporation is going to do business in states other than Nevada, you may want to check to see if your corporate name is being used in those states. You may be prohibited from registering your Nevada corporation in the other state(s) if your corporate name is being used there.

> YOU CAN RESERVE A CORPORATE NAME WITH THE SECRETARY OF STATE FOR A PERIOD OF NINETY DAYS.

If you're searching for a new name unlike any others, include a Spanish, French, or any foreign word in the name and you will be safe. Try to have the name in some way reflect the activities of the corporation. For instance, if your Nevada corporation is going to hold "friendly liens" on your real estate holdings, call the company "ABC Mortgage Company" or something similar.

After forming your corporation, you must pay a nominal fee each year to the secretary of state to file the annual list of officers and directors to keep the company in good standing. If you fail to make this filing and the list is between 60 and 270 days late, it lapses into a "delinquent status" or DQ on the Web site. Delinquent corporations may be brought current any time during this period by paying a nominal penalty fee in addition to the already low annual fee. It is important to have a diligent registered agent for your corporation because they will receive the only notice from the secretary of state of a corporation's failure to file the annual list of officers and directors. In our office we have a tickler system on computer to automatically send our clients three separate notices if their corporation has failed to file the annual list.

If, for any reason, a corporation has not been brought into compliance within nine months after the annual list is due, the corporate charter will be revoked (RV) by the state. A corporation that has been revoked may be reinstated anytime within five years by paying all the fees that applied during the delinquent period plus a small reinstatement fee. However, during the five year period of revocation, anyone may form a new corporation and swipe your corporate name precluding you from reviving your company. Further, anytime your corporation is in the revoked status, the corporate veil protecting any individuals from personal liability is gone.

Sometimes a bank, title company, or lender will want confirmation that your company is in good standing. For a nominal sum, the secretary of state will issue you a "certificate of good standing" for your corporation assuming all

> FOR A NOMINAL SUM, THE SECRETARY OF STATE WILL ISSUE YOU A "CERTIFICATE OF GOOD STANDING."

the filing requirements are current. Anytime you register your corporation in another state you can expect the new state to require this certificate.

Finally, like many states, Nevada has adopted the small corporate offering resolution form (SCOR Form U-7) allowing a business to raise capital through a public offering of up to $1 million every twelve months. This program has been approved by the Securities and Exchange Commission and the American Bar Association. It works as an exemption from federal registration in accordance with Rule 504 of regulation D of the federal securities code. The program is designed for small companies to raise a limited amount of capital without the burdensome expense and paperwork of a full-blown public offering.

Summary

If privacy is the cornerstone of any asset protection plan, Nevada is the place to start. I love the Internet, but the reckless dissemination of people's personal data is unstoppable. You have to assume that any document in the outside world with your name on

> IF PRIVACY IS THE CORNERSTONE OF ANY ASSET PROTECTION PLAN, NEVADA IS THE PLACE TO START.

it can be found. Nevada corporate law provides the best legal entity to form the first line of defense, but there are instances where you may want protection beyond any collection agency, private investigator, lawyer, or angry spouse.

In the event you are a party to a federal lawsuit or in a dispute with a federal government agency such as the IRS or customs service, you may want the maximum asset protection afforded by an offshore corporation. An offshore corporation operates very much like a Nevada corporation, except there is greater privacy and your assets are shielded from capricious federal judges and any government agency.

In the next chapter we'll take a look at using offshore corporations when maximum asset protection is necessary.

Chapter 5
The Tax Savings Advantages of a Nevada Corporation

Wherever you live, whatever you do, there may be ways to reduce your tax liability by using one or more Nevada corporations. I urge you to consult an accountant or other tax expert for specifics, but here are a few areas where tax savings may be available to you:

1. There are no state corporate income taxes in Nevada.

2. There are no state personal taxes in Nevada.

3. A Nevada corporation pays only 15% federal tax on the first $50,000 of income. Compare this to the federal tax rate of 28% on the first $50,000 of personal income.

4. You may be able to use your Nevada corporation to pay your travel and entertainment expenses.

5. Your Nevada corporation may be able to pay your automobile expenses or purchase your car giving you both asset protection and possible tax savings.

6. You may be able to reduce your taxes by placing family members, including minor children, on the corporate payroll.

7. Your Nevada corporation can establish a Pension and Profit Sharing Plan to be fully funded by the corporation for retirement purposes.

8. You may be able to greatly reduce your self-employment taxes (FICA) with a Nevada corporation.

9. You may be able to use your Nevada corporation to pay all your medical bills as a totally deductible corporate expense.

10. Owning a Nevada corporation may be able to reduce any Workmen's Compensation expenses you may have.

11. You may be able to reduce your tax liability by paying all of your child's college expenses from a Nevada corporation.

12. You can eliminate any double taxation by investing any excess corporate profits in new business ventures, investments, a second home or other real estate.

13. You may be able to shift your personal income to multiple Nevada corporations owned by separate family members to take advantage of the lower corporate tax taxes on the first $50,000 of corporate income as mentioned above.

14. You may be able to have your Nevada corporation own a condominium as a business location to maximize your tax deductions.

15. You may be able to use your Nevada corporation to open a stock brokerage account to reduce taxes and provide asset protection.

16. In some cases, you can shift all or part of your gross profits from a tax state to tax-free Nevada by using a Nevada corporation.

17. Foreign nationals with no Social Security numbers can use a Nevada corporation to pay income tax.

18. You can qualify your Nevada corporation as a Subchapter S corporation allowing you to withdraw money from the corporation as a non-taxable dividend from the corporate accumulative earnings account.

We refer clients of our company to an experienced CPA firm in Las Vegas, Nevada, for qualified tax advice concerning Nevada corporations. They will also prepare and file any applicable federal tax returns in a timely manner.

CHAPTER 6

MAXIMUM ASSET PROTECTION

The Offshore Corporation

Remember my lunch with the federal Judge in Chapter 1 when he said, "If I can find an asset within my jurisdiction, I can seize it." His jurisdiction is the United States and its territories. Outside the United States, however, Mr. All-Powerful Judge has no power, standing, or jurisdiction.

In 1996, we elected a president accused of rape, sexual assault, perjury, suborning perjury, and obstruction of justice. . . he not only didn't get indicted, but he kept his job! A Marine Corps pilot buzzes a gondola in Italy and kills twenty innocent people. . .

> OUTSIDE THE UNITED STATES, MR. ALL-POWERFUL JUDGE HAS NO POWER, STANDING, OR JURISDICTION.

and he walks. O.J. literally walks the fairways of southern Florida. It's easy to understand why other countries are wary, if not outright distrustful, of the U.S. government and its judicial system.

Historically, the U.S. government has always bullied smaller countries, from Vietnam to Grenada to Serbia, with our military might or the threat of terminating financial aid. Our foreign policy is, "Do what we say or we will bomb you." This has caused a certain level of unspoken resentment towards the U.S. government in its self-appointed role as Big Brother. There is no question the U.S. would have liberated (see: colonized) Cuba long ago but for the threat of a nuclear war. As long as the United Nations and the concept of sovereignty for individual nations still exists, the concept of offshore asset protection will not only continue to exist, it will grow exponentially. As the loss of privacy escalates and the size of the federal bureaucracy grows, more Americans will look outside our borders to protect their assets from the arbitrary actions of our federal government and the U.S. courts.

In a related development, the growth of the Internet has diminished some of our xenophobia and made people less reluctant to deal with foreign countries, especially when it comes to Web site sales and commerce. You don't hear any Web site owner bemoaning the fact that foreigners are buying their products on the Web with a credit card. We've been raised to believe any economic system, bank, or currency outside the U.S. is inferior to ours. Of course this is still true in some parts of the world, but as the velocity of money and international commerce increases, the concept of moving money offshore for asset protection will become commonplace.

> YOU DON'T HEAR ANY WEB SITE OWNER BEMOANING THE FACT THAT FOREIGNERS ARE BUYING THEIR PRODUCTS ON THE WEB WITH A CREDIT CARD.

The days of speaking to someone in Nassau on a scratchy, double-echo phone line are over. E-mail, coded faxes, and encrypted software designed to protect the privacy of all our offshore communications are here to stay. Computers and the Internet give all of us in the asset protection business a leg up on the government. Like any bully, they're big and powerful, but they're slow.

For most people, a series of Nevada corporations with an experienced nominee will adequately protect their assets. However, if you've been targeted by the IRS, or are routinely involved in litigation, or have accumulated liquid assets over $250,000, an offshore corporation should be part of your asset protection plan.

I have a friend here in Las Vegas we'll call Rick. Rick is a professional card player. His game is blackjack. . . and he's good. He's a young, handsome, Latino kid (he's over 21) with a penchant for playing three or four boxes at $5,000 a hand.

Rick is cocky, but he is not a crook. We all understand that casino gambling is a "privilege" allowing casino owners to kick out anyone they don't like, but no casino owner wants the reputation of being afraid to take on high stakes players (especially cocky, young, handsome Latino kids). So Rick has drawn the attention of the pit bosses in their shiny suits and bad haircuts. Recently, Rick has been on a roll with wins of over $20,000 several times in a row at different casinos. Casino bosses are a cliquish (I did not say greedy) bunch so they began comparing notes on the style of Rick's play. Is he counting cards? (Of course, and they know that.) Is he colluding with a dealer? (No way, their "eyes in the sky" would've seen it.) Or is he just good? And probably lucky. This makes them nervous, so they have asked a professional investigation agency to check up on Rick. One casino has held $100,000 of his winnings "pending the outcome of the investigation." They've checked with his former employers, his former girlfriends, and his friends looking for dirt. They've found nothing because there's nothing to find, so now they have appealed to the federal bank regulators to look at Rick's cash transactions. To deposit or withdraw over $10,000 in cash from a bank or casino cage requires the filing of a currency transaction report (CTR) that is filed with all appropriate federal agencies. These reports are a nuisance for both the player and the casino. The casinos hate to see any player spend time preparing a government report when he could be working the tables, so they routinely ignore the CTR's if at all possible. Except with Rick.

The feds are now looking (literally) at the size and frequency of Rick's cash withdrawals by reviewing the casino video tapes and the cashiers' records of various casinos. They are hoping to build a 'structuring' case against Rick at the behest of the casino owners so they can kick him out as an alleged criminal and avoid the negative publicity of admitting they can't handle a young, cocky, handsome, Latino with extraordinary skills. "Structuring," you may remember, is a felony whereby a person knowingly organizes (structures) his cash transactions in sums of less than $10,000 to avoid having to file a CTR.

> "STRUCTURING," YOU MAY REMEMBER, IS A FELONY.

Rick is smart at things other than cards. Rick has a clean, taxpaying Nevada corporation that no one knows about, but now that the feds are involved , Rick has quietly moved his liquid assets to his corporate offshore bank accounts that were established long before any investigation was instigated. Without question, his Nevada corporation has provided him with the asset protection and privacy he desired, but Rick has heard about my lunch with my friend the federal judge, and his "if I can find'em I can seize'em" philosophy on taking people's assets. With this in mind, he felt it was prudent (and easy) to place his assets beyond the reach of any federal judge or governmental agency. They may never find, pierce, or seize the assets of his Nevada corporation, but these facts are a good example of a situation where maximum asset protection is warranted. If Rick stays out of the casinos for awhile, chances are the investigation will fade away. In any event, both his assets and peace of mind have been fully protected.

Selecting an Offshore Haven

In 1990, when I entered the asset protection business, I traveled to all the offshore havens I had ever read about. From London to Liechtenstein, from the Bahamas to Singapore, I visited over forty separate countries and spoke with (or tried to speak with) local bankers and attorneys.

Primary Language

English is the only language I speak fluently. Oh, sure, I can order dinner (sort of) in Rome or Paris, but when it comes to discussing money, communication is critical. Ordering the wrong wine is not the same as asking for a six month time deposit and getting a six year time deposit. I strongly advise clients to use an offshore haven where everyone speaks fluent, understandable English and where all of their documents are printed in English in addition to any other language.

USE AN OFFSHORE HAVEN WHERE
EVERYONE SPEAKS FLUENT,
UNDERSTANDABLE ENGLISH.

All of the bankers in central Europe speak English in addition to several other languages. Because English is one of the romance languages, you can usually figure out the meaning of signs, brochures, and advertisements in French and Spanish without being a UN interpreter. So, as a general statement, there is no language barrier in using any of the central European counties as an offshore haven.

Most of the bankers and financial services people in the island nations in the Caribbean speak excellent English. All bankers in China, Japan, Malaysia, and Thailand claim to speak English, but when you talk on the phone things get muddy. Bangkok is a beautiful place to visit, but when they get excited and say, "Yew maka vely mucha goot mooney wit dis plaas," it makes a guy nervous. Translated, this means, "You can make excellent interest on your money if you place it with our bank."

People in Singapore, however, speak perfect English, and that's part of the reason they serve as the financial clearing house in the Orient.

Choice of Governing Law

Again, in the interest of keeping things somewhat familiar, I prefer countries that use a legal system patterned after the British common law. This means the system is based on a system of equity, with codified statutes, and separate civil and criminal codes.

In many countries the line separating a civil and criminal wrong is blurry. For instance, in countries like Malaysia, for what we would think

> I PREFER COUNTRIES THAT USE A LEGAL SYSTEM PATTERNED AFTER THE BRITISH COMMON LAW.

of as a simple breach of contract giving rise to a civil law suit, you may be placed in jail or have your assets seized until you explain why you didn't fulfill your end of the agreement – especially if you're not a Malaysian citizen. I'm not concerned about the court system in an offshore haven because I never intend to litigate there, but the government should have an economic incentive to see that your money is protected.

Select an Independent Country

Make sure the offshore haven you're considering is not subject to any laws of a parent country. Some island nations are not really sovereign countries, they are protectorates operating loosely under the jurisdiction of a larger, stronger country. An offshore haven must not have any compromising treaties with the U.S. making it susceptible to U.S. government influence. In the past twenty years, the U.S. has cut back on foreign aid, reducing its ability to pressure independent countries to cooperate on the exchange of financial information.

In addition to being an independent country, a favorable offshore haven must be in the business of providing asset protection, banking secrecy, and refusing to honor foreign court judgments. Offshore banking should be a significant percentage of any offshore haven's gross national product, providing them with an incentive to protect their clients' privacy and money.

Check the Infrastructure of the Offshore Haven

Make sure you can call your offshore banker from any cellular or pay phone using a prepaid phone card. Visit a Kinko's or other public fax machine and exchange faxes with your offshore attorney to make sure there are no glitches. Costa Rica, for example, has great beaches, but many of their attorneys don't have fax machines forcing them to visit a bank to accept or receive a fax, causing delays.

> MAKE SURE YOU CAN CALL YOUR OFFSHORE BANKER USING A PREPAID PHONE CARD.

If it's important to you, make sure your offshore banker is on the Internet and can transmit e-mail without interruption. Personally, I do not recommend using the Internet for any private financial information unless you are using encrypted software. Bill Gates is the richest and certainly one of the smartest guys around, but when the Justice Department took Microsoft to court, the government located and produced every scrap of e-mail he'd ever sent. Scott McNealy, CEO of Sun Microsystems, was asked if there was any way Internet users could protect the exchange of personal information. He replied, "You already have zero privacy – get over it."

If you're truly concerned about telephone privacy, you can buy a digital phone with high-quality voice encryption from Cylink, Motorola, and other companies.

Test your offshore bank with a wire transfer. Make sure it's received and credited promptly. Check how long it takes for a letter to arrive in your offshore bank. Ease of communication, especially if you're ever in the throes of a financial crisis, will give you peace of mind.

Political and Economic Stability

Review the general economic and political history of any offshore haven. Is the government stable, subject to overthrow, corrupt? Is the currency of the country stable?

Central European countries have a long history of managing and protecting people's money. Most Caribbean offshore centers are reliable. But some of them have only recently entered the offshore asset protection business in hopes of imitating the success enjoyed by neighbor countries such as the Bahamas.

China, Malaysia, and Thailand are examples of growing, industrious economies that you may want to invest in, but they are unsuitable as offshore havens due to their political instability. Singapore is the only place in the Orient to use as an offshore haven, if you're working on that side of the world.

Treaties between the
Offshore Haven and the U.S.

Ask your offshore banker point blank, "Do you ever share any banking information with the IRS or any U.S. government agency?" The Bahamas, as the best example, has passed a bank secrecy act specifically prohibiting the disclosure of any banking information to outside sources, including the U.S.

Almost all offshore havens, even the best ones, have agreed not to launder money for known drug dealers or other criminals. However, most offshore centers, even those that have signed the Mutual Legal Assistance Treaty (MLAT) providing for the exchange of information among its members, specifically exclude any tax crimes or tax evasion in their definition of "crime," allowing them to protect the secrecy of their clients. In other words, almost every country outside the U.S. does not view tax evasion as a crime.

> THE BAHAMAS HAS PASSED A BANK SECRECY ACT SPECIFICALLY PROHIBITING THE DISCLOSURE OF ANY BANKING INFORMATION.

In Europe, tax evasion is viewed as a sport more than a crime. In socialistic Scandinavia, you can routinely meet regular, everyday business people that have spent 30 to 120 days in jail for failing to pay their onerous tax bills. They view these incidents in the same manner we view speeding tickets. It's against the law, but the violator is not viewed as a threat to society. It's ironic that only in the most prosperous, supposedly democratic nation in the world do we have an IRS that views anyone failing to pay their taxes as a criminal posing a threat to society.

Local Customs and Social Environment

Choose an offshore haven that you enjoy visiting and can be reached relatively easily. If you have to break out a world atlas and a compass to find an offshore haven, that doesn't make it any more secret than anyplace else, it just probably means you'll never go there.

> CHOOSE AN OFFSHORE HAVEN THAT YOU ENJOY VISITING AND CAN BE REACHED RELATIVELY EASILY.

Check the local tax laws, real estate ownership, securing a work permit, and whether they offer a second passport. There may be certain additional benefits of a particular haven that fit your needs. Meet with a local attorney, money manager, or accountant and check out other financial services.

If you like the weather, the people, and the physical environment, odds are you'll "visit your money," as European bankers like to say, once each year.

Review of the Most Popular Offshore Havens of the World

Below is my subjective review of most of the better known offshore havens. Our company uses all of the havens listed below for specific needs, and each of them has a role to play in the asset protection business. In my opinion, the best place to form an offshore corporation is the Bahamas, so let's start with them.

1. The Bahamas

The Bahamas became an independent nation within the British Commonwealth of Nations on July 10, 1973. It has a tripartite political system with a Ministerial Cabinet, Parliament, and Senate similar to the three branches of government used by the United States. English is the official language and English common law prevails, amended by local statutes.

There are virtually no taxes on foreigners placing their money there. There are no corporate, personal, income, capital gains, profits, sales, inheritance, or estate taxes. There are no withholding taxes on dividends, interest, royalties, or payroll taxes. There are no taxes on foreign-earned income.

> THERE ARE VIRTUALLY NO TAXES ON FOREIGNERS.

The Bahamas Bank and Trust Company Regulatory Act prohibits, under penalty of law, the disclosure of information pertaining to a client's affairs to a third party without the customer's written permission. This is commonly called the bank secrecy act. One of their government publications covering the banking industry in the Bahamas states flatly, "Tax evasion is not illegal in the Bahamas, since we do not have income, capital gains, or inheritance taxes. Tax evasion is not considered suitable grounds for ordering access to information about an account." The Bahamas does not recognize any foreign court judgments. The

Bahamas has had their bank secrecy legislation tested on many occasions and has come through beautifully each time.

Recently, a U.S. federal court in Manhattan levied a fine of almost $2 million dollars against an investor using an offshore corporation as his trading entity who was a client of the Royal Bank of Canada in Nassau. The court claimed the investor had profited illegally from trading options of Duracell International just prior to Duracell being bought by the Gillette Company. The court seized $603,275 in an account located in the U.S. The SEC asked the Royal Bank of Canada to disclose the name of the individual investor who ordered the trades through their bank. The bank cited their bank secrecy laws and refused to disclose the name of the beneficial owner of the corporate account. The Royal Bank was not accused of any wrongdoing. The SEC and the court admitted they would probably be unable to collect the fine "unless we find there are assets we can reach." The bank admitted they would no longer do business with this particular investor, but they never at any time revealed his identity or allowed any of his assets to be seized. On June 10, 1993, Mr. Orville A. Turnquest, Minister of Justice and Foreign Affairs, stated, "Bahamas is not only committed to the bank secrecy laws, but to the prevention of intrusion by foreign governments." The Bahamas has over four hundred banks specializing in providing privacy, asset protection, and money management. The offshore banking business and related services comprises almost 50 percent of its gross national product – with tourism providing the rest. Nassau and Freeport are frequent stops for U.S. cruise ships.

They are in the U.S. Eastern time zone and have excellent phone and communication services. The Bahamas have enacted the International Business Companies Act patterned after the successful British Virgin Islands act, allowing the easy and inexpensive creation of an international business company better known as an offshore corporation. Nominee officers and directors are allowed and may open corporate bank accounts.

Nassau is just sixty miles from Miami with convenient airline connections to anywhere in the world. Telephone calls to and from the Bahamas may be dialed directly. With beautiful beaches and a balmy year around temperature of 72 degrees, the Bahamas is a delightful location to visit on business or pleasure and an ideal retirement location.

> NASSAU IS JUST SIXTY MILES FROM MIAMI WITH CONVENIENT AIRLINE CONNECTIONS TO ANYWHERE IN THE WORLD.

2. Aruba

Aruba is an island nation located just off the northern coast of Venezuela and is part of the Dutch legal system. This country is routinely suspected of laundering money for the drug cartels, if for no other reason, because of its close proximity to Columbia. As a result, they have passed new laws eroding their bank secrecy. Banks are now required to report any "unusual transactions," which could mean anything.

3. Barbados

Barbados is a 166 square mile island nation at the most easterly end of the Caribbean islands, located north and east of Grenada. People speak English and Bajan Creole. The first inhabitants were Arawak and Carib Indians, with English subjects arriving in 1625 and claiming the island for King James I. Soon after, English settlers arrived to grow sugar cane and brought in slaves from Africa to work the fields.

They moved towards becoming an independent country by freeing the slaves in 1834, franchising women in 1944, and codifying a two-party political system and cabinet government in the 1950s. Barbados was granted independence and became a sovereign nation on November 30, 1966.

Barbados does not have any bank secrecy legislation. All bank accounts are open to government inspection, but some confidentiality can be maintained with the use of an international business corporation (IBC). An audit by an independent auditor who is a member of the Institute of Chartered Accountants of Barbados is required each year.

> BARBADOS DOES NOT HAVE ANY BANK SECRECY LEGISLATION.

4. Belize

Belize is located on the east coast of Central America bordering Mexico to the north and Guatemala to the west and south. The population is around 250,000 with approximately 60,000 living in Belize City. People speak English and Spanish.

Up until 1973, Belize was known as British Honduras. It became an independent republic on September 21, 1981. Because of the balmy climate and inexpensive cost of living, many Americans live all or part of the year there. You must live in Belize one year to be granted permanent residency. You may renew your visa every thirty to ninety days until residency is granted. Belize has strict bank secrecy laws that prohibit the disclosure of information. Further, it provides for criminal penalties of up to $50,000 and a prison term of up to one year for any disclosure concerning the business affairs of a client. However, these secrecy laws do not apply to any activities considered crimes in Belize, such as illegal drug activities, theft, or fraud.

Further, on occasion, Belize has released confidential information to U.S. tax authorities through an informal exchange of information agreement. Whenever you see Central American countries hit by a deadly hurricane followed by an offer of financial aid from the U.S., you can be sure the U.S. Government will expect more than a "thank you" when the IRS wants information on U.S. citizens' financial activities there.

Generally speaking, Belize is politically stable, but a British military garrison is stationed there to protect it against periodic threats from Guatemala.

5. Bermuda

Bermuda is not an independent nation. Bermudians are proud of the fact that their country is the oldest British colony. Bermuda is actually 150 small islands, the seven largest connected by bridges and causeways, all located waaay out in the Atlantic over 570 miles off the north Carolina coast and 775 miles southeast of New York.

> **BERMUDA IS NOT AN INDEPENDENT NATION.**

Bermuda has no bank secrecy laws. In fact, Bermuda entered into a tax treaty with the United States in 1986 allowing all of our law enforcement agencies access to any financial information concerning U.S. civil and criminal tax cases.

It's a lovely place to visit for a few days.

6. The British Virgin Islands (BVI)

The British Virgin Islands (BVI) are made up of more than sixty islands, cays, and rocks spread over fifty miles in the Caribbean ninety miles east of Puerto Rico. The population is around 12,000 and the main language is English.

On November 16, 1493, while on his way to Puerto Rico, Christopher Columbus "discovered" the islands. As comedian Dick Gregory has pointed out, how do you "discover" a place where people are already living? In fact, the island was inhabited by Carib Indians.

The BVI became a self-governing colony with their own constitution in 1967. The BVI has excellent bank secrecy laws prohibiting the unauthorized disclosure of any information of a client's affairs to any third party. Tax evasion is not considered a criminal offense in the BVI, so this does not serve as an exemption to their broad secrecy laws. There are no taxes on any income earned outside the islands.

THE BVI BECAME A SELF-GOVERNING COLONY WITH THEIR OWN CONSTITUTION IN 1967.

The BVI is best known among offshore specialists as a leader in writing new and innovative laws pertaining to offshore entities. Specifically, there are two types of companies that can be incorporated in the BVI. The companies act was designed to create corporations to be operated within the BVI, carrying on business with persons in the BVI. The International Business Companies Act of 1984 governs the creation of international business companies (IBCs) for nonresidents doing business outside the BVI. The IBC act, copied by many offshore jurisdictions including the Bahamas, established some of the first asset protection characteristics of what is generally referred to as an "offshore corporation" in the context of asset protection for U.S. citizens. This act allows for bearer shares, requires only one person to serve in all positions of officer(s) and director(s), and the only public record of an IBC consists of the current certificate of incorporation, the memorandum and articles of association, the name and address of the local registered agent, and the record of payments of annual fees (currently about $330 a year).

The BVI has a good infrastructure and would always make my short list of best offshore havens. The only drawback with the BVI is their cozy relationship with the U.S. government. In 1987, the BVI signed an exchange of information agreement with the U.S. allowing bank accounts to be examined if there is evidence of them being used for drug trafficking or money laundering. On its face, this agreement is not so unusual or detrimental to asset protection. However, in the 1980s, when the SEC broke up insider trading on Wall Street, the BVI cooperated fully in disclosing banking information pertaining to alleged inside traders. This has always spooked me and others in the asset protection business. Since that time, in the hope of regaining their revered status as an offshore haven, the BVI has written some new laws and waged an effective public relations campaign designed to recover their luster.

7. The Cayman Islands

The Cayman Islands are comprised of three small islands located south of Cuba. The islands have a total area of a hundred square miles, populated by about 30,000 people with most of them living on Grand Cayman. The climate is perfect with an average temperature of 82 degrees in summer and 72 degrees in winter. The ocean is a beautiful blue with bathtub warm temperatures. Everyone speaks English and the streets are lined with banks, brokerage houses, and related financial services companies.

> THE CAYMANS PROVIDE EXCELLENT CUSTOMER SERVICE WITH ABSOLUTE PRIVACY.

The Cayman Islands confidential relationships law prohibits the unauthorized disclosure of information pertaining to a clients' affairs. The act sets out criminal penalties of fines or prison terms for any disclosure of information concerning the business affairs of any banking or brokerage house client. This law applies to all government officials as well.

The Caymans provide excellent customer service with absolute privacy, money market accounts, and easy communication on the telephone and the Internet. Although we use Bahamian corporations because they are accepted worldwide, we currently open most of our corporate offshore accounts at a brokerage house in the Caymans. The accounts are insured, account information is accessible on the Internet, and our broker can open a numbered corporate account in less than a week.

8. The Channel Islands

The Channel Islands – Guernsey and Jersey are the two main islands surrounded by other smaller islands including Alderney, Herm, and Sark. Each of the Channel Islands operates independently, but they are all considered dependent territories of the English Crown, owing their allegiance to the monarch, although they have no direct link with parliament.

Guernsey is located eighty miles south of England with a population of approximately 55,000. Guernsey has no written bank secrecy laws. Secrecy is assured by the common law principle of confidentiality. One of the bankers on Guernsey told me, "Guernsey does not have any exchange of information treaties with the United States and our clients' privacy is central to the preservation of our offshore status."

Jersey is the largest of the Channel Islands at sixty-two square miles with a population of over 85,000. It is located just twelve miles from the coast of Normandy and the official language is French. The biggest problem is the requirement to file an annual tax return and pay a 20 percent income tax unless the company is exempted, allowing it to pay a flat annual tax of approximately $1,000.

> THE CHANNEL ISLANDS SERVE AS A CONVENIENT OFFSHORE HAVEN FOR THE PEOPLE OF ENGLAND AND FRANCE.

The Channel Islands serve as a convenient offshore haven for the people of England and France. They are difficult to get to and a letter or fax takes weeks, the phone lines are scratchy, and the people retain a certain level of arrogance when dealing with Americans. For these reasons, I don't recommend the Channel Islands to anyone.

9. The Cook Islands

The Cook Islands are made up of fifteen islands scattered in the South Pacific north and east of New Zealand and east of the Samoas. Most of the 20,000 people live in Avarva on Rarotonga Island, and English is the principal language. The islands were a British protectorate before 1891 when they were annexed into New Zealand territory. To this day islanders hold New Zealand citizenship. The islands became self governing under a Westminster model constitution in 1965.

In 1981, Australian David Lloyd established the Cook Islands as an offshore haven. In 1982, he was successful in getting the government to pass laws allowing international business corporations and trusts.

Tax evasion is not a crime in the Cook Islands and there are no taxes on nonresidents not doing business in the islands. They have strict bank secrecy laws which apply to everyone, including government officials. There are no tax treaties between the Cook Islands and the United States, but indirectly the islands are bound by the Income Tax Convention of 1948 between New Zealand and the United States.

Generally speaking, the Cook Islands are a respectable, efficient offshore haven. My only concern is their cozy relationship with New Zealand. The United States and New Zealand are staunch allies and a general air of cooperation exists between the countries, giving rise to possible breaches of the bank secrecy laws if the United States pressured them.

10. Gibraltar

Gibraltar is a British colony on the Rock of Gibraltar located on the southern coast of Spain at the opening between the Atlantic Ocean and the

Mediterrean Sea. The Rock itself is composed of limestone and rises over 1,300 feet in height. Gibraltar comprises only 2.5 square miles and faces North Africa twenty miles across the strait. The 35,000 residents speak English and Spanish. Gibraltar was ceded by the Spanish to the English in 1713 making it a British Crown Colony. Since 1965, it has been a self-governing British colony as a result of their 1965 constitution. To this day, Spain is upset they gave Gibraltar to the British, and periodically threatens to take it back.

All banks are under the purview of the Gibraltarian Banking Authority and are subject to specific legislation guaranteeing anonymity for all banking clients. Nonresidents are tax exempt and there are no tax treaties between Gibraltar and the United States.

The only problem with Gibraltar, as with many of the offshore havens listed here, is that it is not a truly independent nation. Gibraltar operates on its own, but it still relies on Britain to set its foreign policy and to provide for its defense. Britain is obviously one of our closest allies, so, once again, the issue of their bank secrecy laws against the might of the U.S. government is open to question.

11. Hong Kong

Hong Kong used to be an excellent offshore haven until June 30, 1997, when the lease with the British expired, causing the whole area to be given back to the Communists. Although they welcome new accounts from Americans, the Communists can, and will, change any rules at any time. There is nothing stopping them from seizing foreign bank accounts, especially if there is diplomatic friction with the United States.

12. The Isle of Man

The Isle of Man is a 227 square mile island in the Irish Sea off the west coast of Britain with a population of over 70,000. The weather is cold, humid, overcast, and windy. They speak English and Gaelic which is virtually impossible to understand. The Brits and the Scots fought over the island for centuries until the 15th century when the isle emerged as an independent sovereign kingdom with its own parliament and king.

Although they have no specific bank secrecy laws, there is an implied contractual duty for all bankers to keep their client information secret and the guarantee of confidentiality is a bank license condition. Any criminal activity, excluding tax investigations, will create an exemption to any secrecy rules they may have. Although they are an independent country, they still rely on the British for handling their external affairs and defense. Again,

> [THE ISLE OF MAN HAS] NO SPECIFIC BANK SECRECY LAWS.

their tight relationship with the UK makes their promises of bank secrecy suspect.

13. Liechtenstein

Liechtenstein, located on the eastern border of Switzerland, has been a completely independent country since 1806. With only 30,000 citizens on a speck of land less than one hundred square miles, the state is ruled by a prince and royal family in the capital city of Vaduz. Banking and money management are the primary businesses of this country. The royal family is the majority shareholder in the Bank of Liechtenstein.

Liechtenstein may be best known for its creation of a unique legal entity called a "family foundation" made famous by convicted Wall Street trader, Michael Milken. When he was indicted on a long list of felonies in New York, alleging he'd committed every crime under the sun, the government investigated the location of his considerable assets. They found he had established a foundation in Liechtenstein, among other things, and reported it to the federal court in New York City. Milken eventually plea bargained and agreed to pay the government millions in fines, but never at any time did tiny little Liechtenstein ever agree to surrender Milken's money to the court. Milken paid his fine, but to this day, to the best of my knowledge, his foundation has never been disturbed.

In spite of this unwanted publicity, Liechtenstein still has some of the best bank secrecy laws in the world. With only a hundred square miles to work with,

> LIECHTENSTEIN STILL HAS SOME OF THE BEST BANK SECRECY LAWS IN THE WORLD.

banking is the heart and soul of their entire economy. Anyone revealing bank account information to a third party is guilty of a criminal offense punishable by jail time. Many of their banks offer a "discreet customer" status allowing all communications with the bank between the customer and the bank to be made only under an agreed password. No names are ever revealed. The customer's name is known only to a select few of the bank's employees.

Banks, however, have agreed as a general rule to determine the actual identity of the beneficial owner of any numbered or corporate account. However, Liechtenstein has recently authorized certain of its citizens to be the holders of "professional secrets," allowing them to hold the actual name of the beneficial owner of any bank account. These specific individuals may submit a declaration to the bank in lieu of the actual identity of the beneficial owner to protect the owner's privacy.

As a result of the Michael Milken fiasco, some banks now require a signed "information waiver" from its customers that reads as follows:

"The undersigned (the Customer) hereby confirms that he will not carry out any transaction concerning his securities account with this Bank which is considered as insider trading not allowed by law or other regulations in that country in which the transaction is carried out. If proceedings against the bank are commenced by the authorities having jurisdiction for investigations in insider trading in the respective countries, the Bank will inform the customer immediately after receipt of a request for information. The Bank reserves the right to take any steps which it may deem appropriate after due consideration and the expiration of 30 days since the forwarding of the information to the Customer. In such case the Customer authorizes the Bank to reveal to the Authorities his name and details of any alleged insider trading. This authorization shall be effective only if proceedings are initiated against the Bank because of insider trading."

In spite of this waiver, Liechtenstein is still one of the best offshore havens in the world, especially for secrecy. There is no income tax on any profits generated outside the country. Everyone in the financial services business speaks at least five languages and is well versed in money management, different currencies, global interest rates, and so on. The bankers are almost painfully modest and close-mouthed. Secrecy is their calling card. Snuggled next to Switzerland, it's a beautiful place to visit with easy access.

14. Nevis and St. Kitts

Nevis and St. Kitts is a small island country in the Lesser Antilles of the Caribbean just southeast of the Virgin Islands. As an independent state it is fast becoming a popular offshore haven. It gained its independence in 1983 from Britain and is a member of the Caribbean Federation of St. Kitts, Nevis, and Anguilla. Nevis is a tiny, beautiful island of just thirty-six square miles whose only businesses are banking and tourism. The Four Seasons Hotel there is considered by many to be the best in the world. The government has recently upgraded their offshore center in St. Kitts by fully computerizing the registration of corporations and trusts.

The Confidentiality Relationship Act of 1985 prohibits the unauthorized disclosure of information pertaining to a clients' affairs to a third party, punishable by a prison term. They will only release information if there is suspected criminal activity such as the sale of drugs, theft, or fraud. They will not release any information to assist any tax investigations. The Business Corporation Ordinance of 1984 governs nonresident domestic corporations.

> THE CONFIDENTIALITY RELATIONSHIP ACT OF 1985 PROHIBITS THE UNAUTHORIZED DISCLOSURE OF INFORMATION PERTAINING TO A CLIENTS' AFFAIRS TO A THIRD PARTY, PUNISHABLE BY A PRISON TERM.

English is spoken and the people in the financial services sector are competent, but everything moves slowly. There's regular time and then there's Caribbean time, a label reserved for specific tropical island countries like Nevis. When you call a lawyer's office in Nevis they'll say, "He's out, he'll be back soon." Doesn't this beg for you to ask, "Out? Where can you go on a rock two miles across?"

Anyway, Nevis is a respectable offshore haven, but it pales in comparison to its Bahamian neighbor located just forty-five minutes from Miami.

15. Panama

Panama, located in Central America, was once regarded as one of the premier offshore havens for Americans until General Noriega got busted, extradited, and imprisoned in Florida. In spite of these troubles, Panama remains a credible offshore haven. After Noriega's departure, they established a truly democratic government and passed laws aimed at attracting foreign investors. They have elections every five years, there are no taxes on income earned outside the country, and beneficial owners of a corporation are not required to be disclosed to the government.

Panama has the Bank Secrecy Law of the Republic of Panama specifically designed to allow numbered (coded) accounts. No one has authority to disclose any information concerning a numbered account under the penalty of fines and a jail sentence.

As part of the agreement with the U.S. to give the Panama Canal back to Panama, their government did agree to forego their secrecy laws if the suspected party is involved in criminal activities such as illegal narcotics, theft, fraud, or related currency violations associated with the crime. This agreement does not allow for exchanging information in matters relating to taxation, however.

The biggest problem with Panama is not its infrastructure or its banking laws, it's their stained reputation as a money launderer for the Columbian drug cartels. At least for the near future, Noriega's conviction has made every transaction in Panama suspect. As a result, if any U.S. government agency alleges any Panamanian account is somehow connected to the drug trade, their secrecy laws could collapse. This uncertainty alone makes Panama unfit for Americans as an offshore haven.

> THIS UNCERTAINTY ALONE MAKES PANAMA UNFIT FOR AMERICANS AS AN OFFSHORE HAVEN.

16. Switzerland

Switzerland is the most famous offshore haven and, due to events in the last few years, probably one of the worst. Since its inception in 1291, armies have been stomping across Switzerland on their way to battle. In 1815, Switzerland declared itself permanently neutral in all European conflicts.

The Swiss claim to have invented the numbered, secret bank account in 1934 with the passage of the Swiss Federal Law Relating to Banks and Savings Institutions. They have strict bank secrecy laws on the books providing for fines and jail time for anyone disclosing any banking information to a third party. Secrecy can be lifted if criminal activity is alleged, but there must be an alleged violation of Swiss criminal law. As with most European countries, tax evasion is not a criminal offense, it is an administrative offense.

The Swiss lost their invincible reputation for bank secrecy in the 1980s case involving Ferdinand and Imelda Marcos. Remember them? She of the 2,000 (or was it 4,000) pairs of shoes. He was the president of the Philippines and had established his own version of a 401k with numbered accounts in Switzerland. No one was surprised that a third world leader had skimmed money from his private fiefdom for his personal stash. It was the amount of money that raised eyebrows. Hundreds and hundreds of millions. A lot of the money came from the foreign aid they had received from the U.S. since the end of World War II.

> THE SWISS LOST THEIR INVINCIBLE REPUTATION FOR BANK SECRECY IN THE 1980s CASE INVOLVING FERDINAND AND IMELDA MARCOS.

So, the United Nations got involved, claiming a violation of Filipino human rights. The United States looked like they'd been duped. Filipinos were starving. So the whole world went looking for the money which was determined to be somewhere in Switzerland.

The United States, without even so much as a court hearing, quickly seized all of the Marcos's assets located in the United States. Imelda also had a bunch of pricey houses around the world, but the motherlode was in Swiss banks. Initially, the Swiss enforced their bank secrecy laws and wouldn't give up any information claiming neutrality, secrecy, and the right of privacy of their customers. The United States responded by initiating the squeeze play and indicted Imelda (Ferdinand was dying so no one cared about him) and all but threatened to bomb the Swiss if they didn't identify the missing funds. The Swiss abandoned their centuries old promises of bank secrecy and eventually disgorged over $590 million dollars belonging to the Marcoses. Don't get me wrong, I'm not suggesting the Marcoses deserved this money. But Imelda was ultimately acquitted on all criminal charges in a U.S. federal court with the help of TV lawyer Gerry Spence (he of the Davy Crockett jacket fame).

For the first time, at least in my lifetime, the Swiss clearly breached their pledge to protect their clients and surrendered the Marcoses and their money to the United States and its allies, in spite of the fact that neither of the Marcoses was ever convicted of any crime. The Swiss immediately defended their actions claiming this breach of secrecy was a once-in-a-lifetime situation involving the leader of a UN country and involved the theft of an ungodly sum of money. Nevertheless, it sent a chill through the asset protection community. And no one liked all the publicity. It was during this period that many new offshore centers in the Caribbean repositioned themselves to fill the breach and attract customers considering new places to protect their money.

In the 1990s, the Swiss reputation was tarnished again with their reluctant and grudging admission that they knowingly kept and protected the assets of Nazis during and after World War II. Initially, they claimed they didn't know the assets belonged to Nazis, until an indisputable paper trail led to their front door. Then it was discovered that a lot of the Nazis and their heirs had died (World War II was dangerous) and the Swiss just sort of sat on the money when no one made a claim. Finally, some of the holocaust survivors traced some of their assets to these accounts, causing the Swiss to surrender at least some of the funds to the survivors.

> THE SWISS REPUTATION WAS TARNISHED AGAIN WITH THEIR ADMISSION THAT THEY PROTECTED THE ASSETS OF NAZIS.

Based on these stories, the Swiss are suspect both legally and morally as an offshore haven. Further, the "Swiss bank account" has become a cliche.

When someone appears to be living beyond their means, people say, "Oh, he probably has his money stashed in a Swiss bank account." Publicity is the antithesis of privacy. No news is good news for any reputable offshore haven and the Swiss are way too famous these days.

17. Singapore

Singapore is the offshore haven of the Orient. It is an island nation located just south of Malaysia in southeast Asia, composed primarily of people of Chinese descent. Just three miles across, tiny little Singapore's sole business is banking and money management. Although they call themselves a democracy, their government has been controlled by one family for a long time. Singapore is probably best known as the country that banned chewing gum (it caused train doors to stick), kicked out *The Wall Street Journal* (they said nasty things about the country), and for the "caning" of a young American man convicted of what amounted to vandalism (some Americans thought this punishment was barbaric).

Everyone speaks English, the climate is humid and tropical, and Singapore Airlines is repeatedly rated as the best airline in the world. So getting there can be painless.

They have strong bank secrecy laws and they do not honor foreign judgments. The Internet has made retrieving and exchanging information with

Singapore quick and easy. In fact, Singapore is the first country to make it a top priority to wire every single home and business for access on the Internet.

The only potential drawback of Singapore is their somewhat dependent relationship with the U.S. government. Although they do not have a specific treaty to exchange information with the U.S., for years they have allowed the U.S. to have a naval base on their shores in consideration for providing them with a military defense, if needed. Nevertheless, at least politically, Singapore's resolve was tested with the "caning" incident. There was tremendous pressure from the U.S. and human rights groups from all over the world to stop the caning, but Singapore patiently explained this was their law and proceeded to cane the hell out of the kid. (He survived nicely.)

> SINGAPORE IS THE OFFSHORE HAVEN OF THE ORIENT.

If, for any reason, you need an offshore haven in the Orient, Singapore is the best and only place. Hong Kong is in Communist hands. Malaysia and Thailand are politically unstable. Vietnam is undeveloped. Japan and Australia have too many ties to the United States.

18. Turks and Caicos

Turks and Caicos are a group of forty islands and cays located in the Caribbean thirty miles southeast of the Bahamas. The two main islands are surrounded by a continuous coral reef, the weather is tropical with low humidity, and the main language is English.

The islands, inhabited by Arawak Indians, were first discovered by Europeans in 1512 by Spanish explorer Juan Ponce del Leon. The Bahamas governed the islands from 1799 to 1848. Then the Turks and Caicos governed themselves for twenty years. Then they were placed under the control of Jamaica until 1962, when they became a self-governing British Crown Colony with a governor appointed by the Queen of England.

The Turks and Caicos have a high degree of client confidentiality. With a population of less than 15,000, their status as an offshore haven is critical to their fragile economy. Professional relationships are protected by the Confidential Relationships Ordinance of 1979 which provides for penalties of $10,000 and imprisonment for up to three years for unauthorized disclosure of confidential information.

> THE TURKS AND CAICOS HAVE A HIGH DEGREE OF CLIENT CONFIDENTIALITY.

They will not reveal any financial information to any foreign government conducting any kind of tax investigation. All IBCs are guaranteed tax exempt status for twenty years from the date of incorporation.

The Turks and Caicos are an excellent offshore haven. Their laws and methods of doing business are very similar to the Bahamas. However, the Bahamas simply have better communication capabilities, they're closer to Miami for ease of travel, and the Bahamas are an independent country. The Turks and Caicos are a British dependency or colony with the controls that status implies.

Offshore Structures

Once you've selected the location of your offshore haven, you've got to decide which offshore structure is best for your particular situation. In the interest of generating excessive fees, most offshore specialists will lecture you, sell you, and try to convince you that what you need is a complete (read: needlessly complex) thorough asset protection plan (read: a series of offshore structures that are redundant and expensive). And for the privilege of *designing* this redundant, expensive Plan they will charge you $10,000, or more.

Offshore asset protection is simply not that complicated. Once your money is beyond the reach of my friend the federal judge, your assets are safe. An offshore corporation is the first and perhaps the only structure you'll ever need. Let's look at the most popular offshore structures.

> ONCE YOUR MONEY IS BEYOND THE REACH OF MY FRIEND THE FEDERAL JUDGE, YOUR ASSETS ARE SAFE.

International Business Company (IBC)

As a starting point in offshore asset protection, I always recommend the formation of an international business company (IBC). After visiting almost all of the offshore havens worldwide, I strongly recommend the use of a Bahamian IBC. Due to poor customer service, I no longer open any bank or brokerage accounts in the Bahamas, but their corporations can be formed in less than a week at an excellent price. Currently, we are using Bahamian IBCs to open corporate brokerage accounts in the Cayman Islands.

The Caribbean style of company act promulgated by the Bahamas has been adopted as a model throughout the world's tax havens for the formation of IBCs. An IBC is a corporation, also referred to as a company, created in an offshore haven, that is authorized to do business worldwide, excluding the country of incorporation. For instance, when a nonresident forms an IBC in the Bahamas, it cannot own real estate there, but it can have bank accounts there.

An IBC is readily accepted in the worldwide banking community as a viable structure to carry on virtually any financial or business venture. Similar to a Nevada corporation, an IBC can do the following:

1. An IBC can promote and market goods and services worldwide unless restricted by the company act of the country of incorporation. These restrictions usually involve offering banking, insurance, or trust services. The Bahamas has virtually no restrictions on the use of an IBC. It

> AN IBC IS READILY ACCEPTED IN THE WORLDWIDE BANKING COMMUNITY AS A VIABLE STRUCTURE TO CARRY ON VIRTUALLY ANY FINANCIAL OR BUSINESS VENTURE.

may be formed for any legal purpose. An IBC may open a U.S. bank account by filing a W-8 form called a Certificate of Foreign Status.

2. An IBC can be both a borrower and a lender. You may choose to borrow money from an IBC. An IBC could be the mortgage holder on your house or any other real estate. The borrower could make payments directly to the offshore IBC bank account and deduct the interest as an expense. Your IBC may also operate as a leasing company. Your IBC can purchase and lease equipment to your domestic company making all lease payments tax deductible.

3. An IBC can purchase or lease real property outside the country of formation. It can also lease personal property like automobiles, boats, office equipment, etc. This allows you to move these items out of your name for asset protection.

4. An IBC can operate as a trading company. For instance, many of my clients use an IBC to set up an Internet business offshore. They advertise their products on the Web, take orders, and even complete fulfillment from the offshore location. Profits are captured in a low tax or no tax environment.

5. An IBC can be used as a marketing, consulting, legal, or financial services company rendering services to U.S. based businesses. Invoices from

the IBC are submitted to your domestic corporation and are paid directly to the offshore bank account of the IBC.

The structure and maintenance of an IBC is similar to a Nevada corporation as well:

1. In the Bahamas, all meetings may be completed by telephone, fax, or e-mail.

2. Bahamian IBCs may issue multiple classes of stock with complete secrecy.

3. With a Bahamian IBC, one person may fill all the officer and director positions, and there are no restrictions on this person's nationality, citizenship, or residency. As with a Nevada corporation, you may use a nominee to serve in all the corporate positions, insuring your total privacy.

> WITH A BAHAMIAN IBC YOU MAY USE A NOMINEE TO SERVE IN ALL THE CORPORATE POSITIONS, INSURING YOUR TOTAL PRIVACY.

4. There is no requirement that any officer or director be a shareholder in the IBC. As a nominee officer only, I have set up hundreds of offshore IBC banking and stock brokerage accounts. The IBC may also have funds professionally managed by a professional money manager. An IBC may be organized as an advertising or marketing company giving you the traditional 15 percent discount on

any advertising purchases by your domestic business.

5. Other legal entities, like another IBC or LLC, may serve as an officer and director of an IBC.

6. There is no requirement to publicly file the names of the directors and officers.

7. In the Bahamas, the corporate books may be maintained outside the country in any place the owners so choose.

8. There are absolutely no taxes on any IBC in the Bahamas so long as the company doesn't conduct business there, exclusive of banking or other financial transactions.

9. You may want to sell your accounts receivable to an IBC for cash, paying only a percentage of their value. The loss could create a tax write-off and the IBC would collect the full amount in a tax free environment.

> MY COMPANY RECOMMENDS A BAHAMIAN IBC ABOVE ANY OTHER OFFSHORE STRUCTURE.

For these reasons, my company recommends a Bahamian IBC above any other offshore structure. Nevertheless, let's look at another offshore option.

The Offshore Asset Protection Trust (APT)

The APT has been the most touted offshore entity in the field of asset protection over the last ten years. Legally speaking, the APT offers absolutely no more asset protection than an IBC. What it does offer is the opportunity for the financial planners, lawyers, and offshore professionals creating the APTs to charge exorbitant fees for the same asset protection that an IBC can provide at a fraction of the cost.

A basic trust is defined as a legal structure in which title to and right of possession of property (the trust "corpus") is in the hands of a third party called the "trustee." The trust is established by the settlor, grantor, or creator. Don't be confused; these words are interchangeable and all mean the same thing.

The person or entity creating the trust and transferring assets to the APT by way of a testamentary disposition or gift (same thing) is the settlor. To be effective, any APT should have minimal contact with the U.S. to avoid being characterized as a U.S. trust.

To protect the integrity of a trust, it is my opinion the settlor should not have the right to directly replace the trustee. The settlor should carefully select a trustee who will follow his general intentions and if, for any reason, the settlor is dissatisfied, will resign quickly. Some trusts have a "standby trustee" in the event the trustee resigns or dies.

When a settlor wants to advise the trustee of his general intentions, he sends the trustee what is called a letter of wishes. This has no legally binding effect, but it does constitute a permissible level of "trustee influence." The key to an effective trust is to remove the legal control and ownership of the trust assets from the settlor. As with a corporation, in a trust, if the settlor is in effect controlling the trustee, the trust may be pierced or set aside causing the assets to be exposed to a legal claim.

The "trust protector" is the person who serves as the watchdog over the trust and the trustee. He makes sure the trustee is doing his job and fulfilling the objectives of the APT. The protector, usually an offshore attorney, provides legally binding counsel and advice to the trustee on interpretation of the trust deed, construing the settlor's letter(s) of wishes, and deciding upon the appropriate action

> THE "TRUST PROTECTOR" IS THE PERSON WHO SERVES AS THE WATCHDOG OVER THE TRUST AND THE TRUSTEE.

after receiving advice from any group of duly appointed advisor(s) to the trust. The protector has "veto" power over any action of the trustee.

The "trustee" is charged with the fiduciary duty of capital conservation and income accumulation for the beneficiaries. A trustee ought not be a U.S. citizen or reside in the United States. Any offshore trustee should be a U.S. nonresident alien making him immune from any U.S. court orders or subpoenas. There may be multiple trustees if the assets (corpus) in the trust are exceptionally large. In this instance, the group of trustees acts like a board of directors for a corporation. (Which begs the question, why not just have a corporation in the first place?)

The beneficiaries, in my opinion, should never include the settlor, even though this is legally permissible. The closer the settlor gets to the assets of the trust, the more likely the trust will be pierced. In many cases there are several classes of beneficiaries, which may include a family foundation (more fees for the attorney forming the APT), a favorite charity, and children born or unborn of the marriage(s) or future marriage(s) of the settlor. A discretionary trust with full powers in the trustee grants the trustee the right to add new beneficiaries and substitute assets of equivalent value.

Any beneficiary may ask for distributions from the trust, but these are made at the sole discretion of the trustee and his interpretation of the trust.

The laws of the offshore jurisdiction will govern the APT. The trust deed should state unequivocally that the trust is to be governed by offshore laws. All trust records should be held in the offshore location or with the offshore trustee.

A committee of investment counselors to the trustee is optional. In these cases, the settlor can be the chairman of the committee with the understanding that the recommendations of the committee are not legally binding on the trustee, merely "advisory" in nature. The trustee's independence must be maintained to protect the integrity of the trust structure.

> THIS CAUSES EVERYTHING TO MOVE SLOWLY AND EXPENSIVELY, MAKING THE OFFSHORE TRUST THE FAVORITE OF FEE-HUNGRY LAWYERS AND FINANCIAL PLANNERS.

In most jurisdictions, the APT is a private document that is not required to be filed or recorded with any government agency. That's the good news – and the bad news. The lawyer who forms the trust is many times selected to be the trustee, and without any public record of the document the settlor must trust him completely. An APT is similar to a signed contract. This is one of the reasons I do not recommend offshore trusts – there are too many people involved with no record of anything should something go wrong. Further, every time you want the trust to do something you have to pay to contact the lawyer, the trustee, the trust protector, the advisory committee, and so on. This causes everything to move slowly and expensively, making the offshore trust the favorite of fee-hungry lawyers and financial planners.

CONCLUSION

Maximum asset protection is accomplished by moving your assets beyond the reach of lawyers, courts, government agencies, and my friend the federal judge. It's not a complicated concept, but if you talk to some of the "offshore specialists" you can spend $50,000 or more on fees forming offshore structures before you move one penny to a safe haven.

If you choose the correct offshore haven with a trusted nominee, the battle is won. If you enjoy complicating your life and spending money, you can have an offshore trust with an offshore corporate trustee with a series of foundations as beneficiaries with a panel of offshore corporations to advise the trustee under the supervision of an offshore law firm with – you get the picture!

Once an asset is out of the reach of my friend the federal judge and the IRS, it's safe. And, even more important, if they never learn the asset is offshore, there's no reason for anyone to talk about it. An offshore international business corporation (IBC) is a legal, time-tested structure that anyone can understand and afford. The annual fees to maintain an IBC are reasonable, and with a nominee officer/director, the beneficial owner can answer honestly and truthfully that he doesn't own or operate the company.

In addition to generating additional fees for forming multiple structures, many people in the asset protection business will tell you that with enough "planning" (read: many expensive trusts, etc.) you will never be obligated to pay taxes again. This is an absolutely false claim. Our income tax system is voluntary, so no one has to pay anything if they don't want to. However, if you're caught and convicted of tax evasion you can be fined and sent to prison. So, the point is this: Are you or any rational person going to tell a Criminal Investigation Division (CID) officer with the IRS or a federal judge, "Listen, you guys, I don't pay taxes because according to my offshore specialist I have organized my financial affairs in an offshore haven with a series of trusts and foundations in a manner making all my income tax free. My offshore advisor is just smarter than you guys. According to the law and their advice, I don't owe any taxes."

True enough, after receiving your fifty-seven months in a federal prison camp, the government won't be able to seize your offshore assets, but there is no IRS agent or federal judge who will agree with you and your (suddenly hard to find) offshore specialist that you have beaten the system and don't owe any taxes.

The IRS will always take the position that any income you or any U.S. citizen earns anywhere in the world is taxable. That is why all of us at Asset Protection Group, Inc. are careful to tell our clients that we are in the asset protection business, not the tax planning business. We guarantee that we can protect your assets from any lawyer or any government agency. We

> THE IRS WILL ALWAYS TAKE THE POSITION THAT ANY INCOME YOU OR ANY U.S. CITIZEN EARNS ANYWHERE IN THE WORLD IS TAXABLE.

can guarantee that the Commonwealth of the Bahamas and the Cayman Islands will not tax your offshore assets so long as you follow their rules. But don't let anyone tell you that they can structure your domestic and offshore entities so that you can safely tell the IRS (and my friend the federal judge) that you have structured your finances so you never owe any taxes. As I tell my clients, what you choose to tell the IRS is like what you choose to tell your priest or rabbi. It's entirely a personal decision with consequences that can only be measured by each individual and his unique set of circumstances.

Asset protection is more than just a legal matter, it involves trust and what I call the "leap of faith." Understanding the domestic and offshore laws that protect your assets is relatively easy. You must also find at least one person to hold, control, and nurture your offshore assets in total confidence.

Only in this way can you answer honestly and truthfully that you do not own or control an IBC or its assets. Only in this way can it be said you are personally separate and distinct from the IBC and its assets.

Only in this way can it be said you have Bulletproof Asset Protection.

ABOUT THE AUTHOR

 William S. Reed, J.D. is President of Asset Protection Group, Inc., a corporation specializing in the area of asset protection. For fifteen years he was an active collection attorney handling over 1,000 lawsuits a month. In 1990, he left the practice of law to develop a system of asset protection for everyday people. He is a highly sought-after speaker known for his dry humor and wit when explaining to people the importance of preserving wealth and protecting assets through the use of Nevada and offshore corporations. Mr. Reed proudly makes his home in the great state of Nevada.